**MFL
AS/A Level**

L'Étranger

Albert Camus

**Oxford
Literature
Companions**

Notes and activities: Simon Kemp

OXFORD

UNIVERSITY PRESS

Contents

Introduction

What are Oxford Literature Companions?

The Oxford Literature Companions (MFL) series
is designed to provide you with comprehensive
support for popular set texts. You can use the
Companion alongside your novel, using relevant
sections during your studies or using the book as a
whole for revision.

Each Companion includes detailed guidance and
practical activities on:

- **Plot and Structure**
- **Context**
- **Characters**
- **Language**
- **Themes**
- **Skills and Practice**

How does the book help with exam preparation?

As well as providing guidance on key areas of the novel, throughout this book you
will also find 'Upgrade' features. These are tips to help with your exam preparation
and performance.

In addition, the **Skills and Practice** chapter provides detailed guidance on areas
such as how to prepare for the exam, understanding the question, planning your
response and hints for what to do (or not do) in the exam. There is also a bank of
Sample questions and **Sample answers**. The **Sample answers** are marked and
include annotations and a summative comment.

How does this book help with terminology?

Throughout the book, key terms are **highlighted** in the text and explained on the
same page with the equivalent term in French. The same terms are included in a
detailed **Glossary** at the end of the book.

Which edition of this novel has been used?

Quotations have been taken from the Gallimard edition of *L'Étranger*
(ISBN 978-207-036002-4) © Éditions Gallimard.

How does this book work?

Each book in the Oxford Literature Companions (MFL) series follows the same approach and includes the following features:

- **Key quotations** from the novel
- **Key terms** explained on the page in English with French translations, linked to a complete glossary at the end of the book
- **Activity boxes** with activities in French to help improve your understanding of the text and your language skills, including:
  - Vocabulary activities
  - Comprehension activities
  - Summary activities
  - Grammar activities
  - Translation activities
  - Research activities
- **Upgrade** tips to help prepare you for your assessment
- **Vocabulary and useful phrases** in French at the end of each chapter to aid your revision

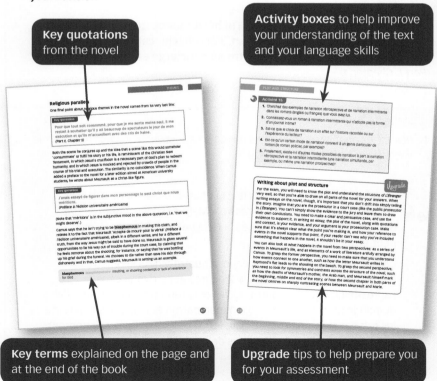

Key quotations from the novel

Activity boxes to help improve your understanding of the text and your language skills

Key terms explained on the page and at the end of the book

Upgrade tips to help prepare you for your assessment

Plot

Première partie

Chapter 1

Meursault receives a telegram from the old people's home in which his mother lives, telling him that she has died. He travels to the home and meets the manager, who tells him not to feel guilty about having put his mother in a home. Meursault, the concierge of the home and some of the residents spend the night watching over his mother's coffin, during which time Meursault drinks coffee and smokes a cigarette. The next morning Meursault walks behind the coffin to the burial in the mounting Algerian heat. M. Pérez, his mother's 'boyfriend', struggles to keep up with the funeral party and collapses at the graveside.

- Meursault's actions here appear trivial, but they will be reinterpreted during his trial to present him as abnormal and heartless.
- Meursault is dominated by physical sensations. Tiredness sends him to sleep on the bus and in the morgue. The light and heat of the sun are unbearable to him.

> **Key quotation**
>
> **J'ai eu alors envie de fumer. Mais j'ai hésité parce que je ne savais pas si je pouvais le faire devant maman. J'ai réfléchi, cela n'avait aucune importance. J'ai offert une cigarette au concierge et nous avons fumé.** *(Part I, Chapter 1)*

Activité 1

1. Relisez les premiers paragraphes du roman attentivement. Vous trouverez le vocabulaire en italiques à la page 25.

> Aujourd'hui, maman est morte. Ou peut-être hier, je ne sais pas. J'ai reçu un télégramme de *l'asile*: « Mère *décédée*. *Enterrement* demain. Sentiments distingués. » Cela ne veut rien dire. C'était peut-être hier.
>
> L'asile de *vieillards* est à Marengo, à quatre-vingts kilomètres d'Alger. Je prendrai l'autobus à 2 heures et j'arriverai dans l'après-midi. Ainsi, je pourrai *veiller* et je rentrerai demain soir. J'ai demandé deux jours de *congé* à mon patron et il ne pouvait pas me les refuser avec une excuse pareille. Mais il n'avait pas l'air content. Je lui ai même dit: « Ce n'est pas de ma faute. » Il n'a pas répondu.

> J'ai pensé alors que je n'aurais pas dû lui dire cela. En somme, je n'avais pas à m'excuser. C'était plutôt à lui de me présenter ses condoléances. Mais il le fera sans doute après-demain, quand il me verra *en deuil*. Pour le moment, c'est un peu comme si maman n'était pas morte. Après l'enterrement, au contraire, ce sera *une affaire classée* et tout *aura revêtu une allure* plus officielle.
>
> J'ai pris l'autobus à 2 heures. Il faisait très chaud. J'ai mangé au restaurant, chez Céleste, comme d'habitude. Ils avaient tous beaucoup de peine pour moi et Céleste m'a dit: « On n'a qu'une mère. » Quand je suis parti, ils m'ont accompagné à la porte. J'étais un peu *étourdi* parce qu'il a fallu que je monte chez Emmanuel pour lui emprunter une cravate noire et *un brassard*. Il a perdu son oncle, il y a quelques mois.
>
> *(Part I, Chapter 1)*

2. Lisez la liste de tous les événements de l'extrait dans l'ordre où ils sont mentionnés dans le texte. Mettez les événements en ordre chronologique, en les numérotant de un à quatorze selon l'ordre dans lequel ils se produisent dans la vie de Meursault. (Attention! Quelques-uns ont peut-être lieu simultanément.)

   a) La mère de Meursault meurt. ☐

   b) Meursault reçoit un télégramme de l'asile. ☐

   c) L'enterrement a lieu. ☐

   d) Meursault prend le bus pour Marengo. ☐

   e) Meursault arrive à l'asile de vieillards. ☐

   f) Meursault veille sur le cercueil. ☐

   g) Meursault revient à Alger. ☐

   h) Meursault demande un congé à son patron. ☐

   i) Le patron de Meursault le voit en deuil. ☐

   j) Il semble à Meursault que sa mère n'est pas vraiment morte. ☐

   k) C'est une affaire classée et tout a revêtu une allure plus officielle. ☐

   l) Meursault déjeune au restaurant de Céleste. ☐

   m) Meursault emprunte une cravate noire et un brassard à Emmanuel. ☐

   n) L'oncle d'Emmanuel meurt. ☐

Chapter 2

Meursault swims and sunbathes at the beach with Marie, a former work colleague, they see a film together at the cinema, and she spends the night at his flat. The next day, he spends the afternoon and evening alone on his balcony, watching the people in the street below.

- Marie is shocked to see Meursault's black tie when he gets dressed, and to learn that he is at the beach so soon after his mother's death. Even characters sympathetic to Meursault can find him unfeeling and his behaviour inappropriate.

- The balcony scene shows Meursault as detached from society. He is happier watching other people than taking part.

- Although nothing much seems to happen in this chapter, it is important as it shows the kind of life Meursault is leading, and the life he would have continued to lead if the events of the next chapter had not started the chain of events that leads to his execution.

Key quotation

Je lui ai dit que maman était morte. Comme elle voulait savoir depuis quand, j'ai répondu: « Depuis hier. » Elle a eu un petit recul, mais n'a fait aucune remarque. J'ai eu envie de lui dire que ce n'était pas de ma faute, mais je me suis arrêté parce que j'ai pensé que je l'avais déjà dit à mon patron. Cela ne signifiait rien.
(Part I, Chapter 2)

Meursault and Marie see a film featuring the famous French comic actor, Fernandel

Activité 2

Reconstruisez la chronologie des premiers jours du roman. Faites correspondre chaque événement au moment où il arrive dans la vie de Meursault.

	Jour		Événement
1	Mercredi ou jeudi	**a**	Meursault veille à l'asile.
2	Jeudi matin	**b**	Meursault rentre à Alger.
3	Jeudi après-midi	**c**	Meursault reste au lit et fume des cigarettes.
4	Nuit de jeudi	**d**	Mort de la mère de Meursault.
5	Vendredi matin	**e**	Meursault et Marie passent la nuit ensemble.
6	Vendredi soir	**f**	Enterrement de la mère de Meursault.
7	Samedi matin	**g**	Meursault reçoit le télégramme et demande un congé à son patron.
8	Samedi soir	**h**	Meursault regarde la rue depuis son balcon.
9	Nuit de samedi	**i**	Meursault rencontre Marie à la plage.
10	Dimanche matin	**j**	Meursault se rend à l'asile.
11	Dimanche après-midi et soir	**k**	Meursault et Marie vont au cinéma.

Exploring other perspectives

To understand the novel, it's important to try to put yourself in the shoes of the people who lived in that time and place, rather than judging things solely from our own perspective. Some things that Meursault does, such as staying up all night to watch over his mother's coffin on the night before the burial, or wearing a black tie and armband in the weeks following the funeral, may seem peculiar. In fact, they are customs that everyone in Meursault's community would share. Conversely, some things he does which seem normal to us, like going to see a comedy film the day after a funeral, are seen as unacceptable by some members of the community. Remember that French **colonial** Algeria in the mid-twentieth century is a very different culture from ours, and notions of appropriate and inappropriate behaviour may not match your own.

colonial *colonial* an area or country which has been conquered and is ruled by another; in this case, the Mediterranean region of Algeria was ruled by France between 1830 and 1962

Chapter 3

Meursault works at the office. Back home, he meets his elderly neighbour, Salamano, who is mistreating and swearing at his dog. Another neighbour, Raymond, invites him in to dinner. Raymond has been in a fight with the brother of his mistress. The brother had learned that Raymond had severely beaten his mistress because he suspected she was cheating on him. Raymond asks Meursault to help him write a letter that will entice his mistress back to his flat. If it works, Raymond plans to spit in her face during sex and throw her out as 'punishment'. Meursault writes the letter for Raymond.

- Salamano's relationship with his dog is described in entirely negative terms. Salamano hates and abuses the dog, which is wretched and terrified.

- Raymond's plan is vile, but Meursault's only comment in agreeing to help him is that he had no reason not to. Meursault is passive, and either does not think deeply or does not care about the morality of his action.

> **Key quotations**
>
> **Alors, ils restent tous les deux sur le trottoir et ils se regardent, le chien avec terreur, l'homme avec haine.**
> *(Part I, Chapter 3)*
>
> **Cela m'était égal d'être son copain [...].**
> *(Part I, Chapter 3)*

Activité 3

Racontez la scène dans l'appartement de Raymond du point de vue de Raymond. Expliquez pourquoi vous voulez que Meursault vous aide et décrivez comment il réagit à votre requête.

Chapter 4

Meursault and Marie spend the next weekend together at the beach and at Meursault's flat. They hear Raymond arguing with his mistress, and then repeatedly hitting her as she screams. A policeman intervenes. Later, Meursault agrees to testify on Raymond's behalf. Salamano has lost his dog. Meursault hears him crying himself to sleep.

- Meursault says nothing when Marie says the assault in Raymond's flat is 'terrible', and he refuses to call the police because, in his words, 'je n'aimais pas les agents' *(Part I, Chapter 4)*. He does nothing to help the woman being abused, but does agree to help her abuser escape justice.

- Salamano's grief at losing his dog makes Meursault think about his mother, although he does not know why, and he is not curious to work out the connection.

> **Key quotation**
>
> La femme criait toujours et Raymond frappait toujours. Marie m'a dit que c'était terrible et je n'ai rien répondu. Elle m'a demandé d'aller chercher un agent, mais je lui ai dit que je n'aimais pas les agents.
> *(Part I, Chapter 4)*

> **Activité 4**
>
> Comment les rapports entre Meursault et Marie sont-ils différents de ceux entre Raymond et sa maîtresse? Donnez quelques exemples tirés des chapitres 2 à 4 pour justifier votre réponse.

Chapter 5

Raymond phones Meursault at work to invite him to spend Sunday at his friend Masson's beach hut. He also tells him that the brother of his mistress, and some other Arab men have been following him around. Meursault receives a proposal from his boss of a posting in Paris and a proposal of marriage from Marie. He is indifferent to both, but agrees to marry Marie, while saying he probably does not love her. Over dinner, Meursault watches a woman behaving like a robot. Back at the flat, Salamano speaks fondly of his lost dog.

- Meursault receives two life-changing offers in one day, but gives them little thought and does not seem to have any emotional response to either of them.

- He agrees to marry Marie in a similar way to how he agreed to write Raymond's letter and testify to the police on his behalf: someone has asked him to do something, and he finds no good reason not to do it, so he accepts.

> **Key quotation**
>
> « Pourquoi m'épouser alors? » a-t-elle dit. Je lui ai expliqué que cela n'avait aucune importance et que si elle le désirait, nous pouvions nous marier. D'ailleurs, c'était elle qui le demandait et moi je me contentais de dire oui. Elle a observé alors que le mariage était une chose grave. J'ai répondu: « Non. »
> *(Part I, Chapter 5)*

> **Activité 5**
>
> Imaginez que vous êtes Marie. Expliquez à une copine ce que vous pensez de Meursault. Racontez comment vous l'avez demandé en mariage et décrivez sa réaction.

Chapter 6

Meursault, Marie and Raymond see a group of Arab men as they are leaving for Masson's beach hut, and Raymond says the brother of his mistress is among them. After sunbathing, swimming and lunch, Masson, Meursault and Raymond are walking on the beach in the midday sun when they see the brother and another man approach. In the fight, one of the Arab men draws a knife and wounds Raymond on the arm. Later, Raymond goes to confront the men with his revolver. Meursault encourages him to fight hand to hand and takes the gun from him, but the Arab men slip away. Meursault accompanies Raymond back to the hut, then returns alone to where the brother, now also alone, is lying by a rock. As the sun beats down on him, and the light reflected from the Arab man's knife blade dazzles him, Meursault fires the gun. He then shoots four more bullets into the man's body.

- The narration leading up to the first shooting suggests Meursault is not fully in control of himself. Emphasis is placed on his extreme physical discomfort in the heat, and the disorienting effect of the sun's glare.

- Meursault does not explain why he shoots four more times, and the implication seems to be that there is no real reason why he does so. Nevertheless, this will become a key part of the prosecution's case that the killing was deliberate and **premeditated**.

> **Key quotation**
>
> **Alors, j'ai tiré encore quatre fois sur un corps inerte où les balles s'enfonçaient sans qu'il y parût. Et c'était comme quatre coups brefs que je frappais sur la porte du malheur.**
> *(Part I, Chapter 6)*

Activité 6

Remplissez les blancs pour compléter ce résumé du dernier épisode du chapitre.

Quand Meursault retrouve l'Arabe, il est allongé sur le ¹_____, son front à l'²_____ d'un ³_____. Son image danse devant les yeux de Meursault à cause de la ⁴_____ de ⁵_____ dans l'⁶_____ enflammé. Meursault entend le bruit paresseux des ⁷_____ et voit un navire à l'⁸_____. La ⁹_____ vibre de ¹⁰_____ et la ¹¹_____ gicle du couteau de l'Arabe. Meursault est aveuglé par la ¹²_____ qui coule dans ses yeux. Il ressent une ¹³_____ de vent brûlante qui vient de la ¹⁴_____ et il lui semble qu'une ¹⁵_____ de feu tombe du ¹⁶_____. Il appuie sur la gâchette du revolver.

air	brume	chaleur	ciel	horizon	lumière	mer	ombre
plage	pluie	rafale	rocher	sable	soleil	sueur	vagues

Deuxième partie

Chapter 1

Meursault has been arrested for the killing, and recounts interviews with the *juge d'instruction* (examining magistrate) and with his lawyer. Both ask him about his mother and are dissatisfied by Meursault's lukewarm expression of feelings for her. Meursault refuses to allow his lawyer to exaggerate how he felt during the funeral. The *juge d'instruction* is frustrated with Meursault's inability to explain his actions on the beach. He brandishes a crucifix, at which point Meursault tells him he does not believe in God, which sends the *juge d'instruction* into a rage. The investigation continues for eleven months, by the end of which the *juge d'instruction* jokingly refers to him as 'monsieur l'Antéchrist' *(Part II, Chapter 1)*.

- Much of the first half of the novel takes place outside, and Camus gives us a sense of open air, space and sunshine. Aside from a brief moment when Meursault is taken from the courtroom to the prison van *(Part II, Chapter 3)*, the entire second half takes place indoors, giving it an atmosphere of oppression and confinement.

- Meursault's honesty becomes an increasingly noticeable and important character trait in this chapter and those that follow. In this chapter, his lawyer tries to persuade him to say something he did not feel, and the *juge d'instruction* tries to bully him into saying something he does not believe. Meursault resists both attempts, even though doing so hurts his own prospects of release.

> **Key quotation**
>
> **Il m'a dit que c'était impossible, que tous les hommes croyaient en Dieu, même ceux qui se détournaient de son visage. C'était là sa conviction et, s'il devait jamais en douter, sa vie n'aurait plus de sens. « Voulez-vous, s'est-il exclamé, que ma vie n'ait pas de sens ? »**
> *(Part II, Chapter 1)*

Activité 7

Du point de vue **a)** du juge d'instruction et **b)** de l'avocat, quelles sont vos premières impressions de Meursault ?

premeditated *prémédité, commis avec préméditation* committed deliberately, having been planned in advance (most often used with reference to murder)

Chapter 2

After an awkward prison visit, Marie writes to Meursault to say she will no longer be allowed to see him as they are not married. Meursault suffers from the loss of freedom, but is **'pas trop malheureux'** *(Part II, Chapter 2)*. He spends his time sleeping, remembering his past life and reading a newspaper article he found in the cell.

- Meursault tells us more about the conversation at the next table than he does about his own conversation with Marie, emphasising how little they have to say to each other.
- The newspaper story has several themes in common with *L'Étranger* itself, including honesty, violence and chance.
- One function of this chapter is briefly to sketch in the uneventful year that passes between the shooting and the start of Meursault's trial.

> **Key quotation**
>
> Elle a crié de nouveau: « Tu sortiras et on se mariera! » J'ai répondu: « Tu crois? » mais c'était surtout pour dire quelque chose.
> *(Part II, Chapter 2)*

Meursault in prison. From Luchino Visconti's 1967 film, *The Stranger*, starring Marcello Mastroianni

Activité 8

1. Relisez le « fait divers » trouvé par Meursault dans sa cellule.

« Un homme était parti d'un village tchèque pour faire fortune. Au bout de vingt-cinq ans, riche, il était revenu avec une femme et un enfant. Sa mère tenait un hôtel avec sa sœur dans son village natal. Pour les surprendre, il avait laissé sa femme et son enfant dans un autre établissement, était allé chez sa mère qui ne l'avait pas reconnu quand il était entré. Par plaisanterie, il avait eu l'idée de prendre une chambre. Il avait montré son argent. Dans la nuit, sa mère et sa sœur l'avaient assassiné à coups de marteau pour le voler et avaient jeté son corps dans la rivière. Le matin, la femme était venue, avait révélé sans le savoir l'identité du voyageur. La mère s'était pendue. La sœur s'était jetée dans un puits. »

(Part II, Chapter 2)

2. Au lieu de citer l'article du journal, Meursault nous raconte l'histoire avec ses propres mots. Essayez de recréer l'article d'origine, écrit dans un style journalistique.

MEURTRE ET DOUBLE SUICIDE EN TCHÉCOSLOVAQUIE

3. Meursault juge « que le voyageur l'avait un peu mérité et qu'il ne faut jamais jouer ». Êtes-vous de son avis? Est-ce que Meursault applique la « leçon » qu'il tire du fait divers à sa propre vie?

Camus later wrote a play, *Le Malentendu*, based on the story recounted in Meursault's newspaper article. It was first performed in 1944

Chapter 3

Meursault's trial begins in a packed and sweltering courtroom. The judge and the prosecutor ask him about the killing and about his mother. The manager and concierge of the old people's home are called as witnesses, as is Thomas Pérez. Meursault's behaviour at the funeral is discussed in detail, with emphasis on the fact he did not know his mother's age and that he smoked a cigarette by her coffin. On the witness stand, Masson, Salamano and Céleste clumsily try to defend Meursault's character. Marie's account of the day after the funeral and Raymond's attempt to blame everything on chance seem to make things worse for Meursault.

- This chapter and the following one essentially retell the story of the first half of the novel. This time, instead of Meursault's account of what happened, we now see events through the eyes of the other characters in the story.

- The accounts of Meursault and his actions are largely controlled and interpreted by the prosecutor examining the witnesses. The prosecutor does everything he can to make Meursault's actions appear deliberate and his character seem heartless.

> **Key quotation**
>
> « [...] j'accuse cet homme d'avoir enterré une mère avec un cœur de criminel. »
> *(Part II, Chapter 3)*

Activité 9

Dans quelle mesure le témoignage des amis et des connaissances de Meursault accable-t-il l'accusé au lieu de l'aider?

Chapter 4

The prosecutor sums up by saying that Meursault premeditated the killing of the Arab man, and returns to the topic of his mother to denounce Meursault as having no soul, no humanity, and no moral principles. Meursault responds that he did not intend to kill the man, and there is laughter in the court as he says it happened 'à cause du soleil' *(Part II, Chapter 4)*. Meursault's lawyer speaks of his 'remords éternel' *(Part II, Chapter 4)* for the killing; Meursault, however, feels the prosecutor was nearer the truth in claiming he felt no regret about his actions. Meursault is brought back into the courtroom to hear the verdict, is found guilty and sentenced to death.

- In this chapter, the prosecutor's flowery and emotive language makes a sharp contrast to the plain language Meursault uses to tell his own story.

- Meursault fails to defend his actions to the court, and declines to offer a response to the judge's verdict at the end of the chapter. This keeps back Meursault's self-justification for the climax of the novel in the following chapter, in his tirade against the chaplain's religious **world view**.

Key quotation

Sans doute, je ne pouvais pas m'empêcher de reconnaître que [le procureur] avait raison. Je ne regrettais pas beaucoup mon acte. Mais tant d'acharnement m'étonnait. J'aurais voulu essayer de lui expliquer cordialement, presque avec affection, que je n'avais jamais pu regretter vraiment quelque chose. J'étais toujours pris par ce qui allait arriver, par aujourd'hui ou par demain.
(Part II, Chapter 4)

 Activité 10

1. Relisez le récit des événements de la première partie du roman selon le procureur, comme Meursault nous les communique.

 J'avais écrit la lettre d'accord avec Raymond pour attirer sa maîtresse et la livrer aux mauvais traitements d'un homme « de moralité douteuse ». J'avais provoqué sur la plage les adversaires de Raymond. Celui-ci avait été blessé. Je lui avais demandé son revolver. J'étais revenu seul pour m'en servir. J'avais abattu l'Arabe comme je le projetais. J'avais attendu. Et « pour être sûr que la besogne était bien faite », j'avais tiré encore quatre balles, posément, à coup sûr, d'une façon réfléchie en quelque sorte.
(Part II, Chapter 4)

2. Analysez le récit:

- Quels éléments du récit traitent de ce que Meursault a fait?
- Quels éléments traitent plutôt de ce que Meursault a pensé, ou des raisons de sa conduite?
- Dans quelle mesure le récit du procureur est-il en accord avec la version des événements racontée par Meursault lui-même? Quels aspects sont différents?

---

world view *la vision du monde* a particular understanding of the world or set of beliefs about life

Chapter 5

Meursault refuses to see the prison chaplain, and thinks about his coming execution, and about chance and inevitability. The chaplain comes in anyway and tries to encourage Meursault to have faith in God and an afterlife. Meursault is provoked into an angry speech about life and death. He says that his certainty about life now and death that will surely follow is worth more than the chaplain's faith in a salvation and afterlife that may not exist. He shouts that the fact that everyone will die makes everyone equal, and means the choices made in life do not matter. When the chaplain has gone, he becomes calmer and more positive. Alone, watching the peaceful starry night through the window of his cell, Meursault feels happiness.

Meursault looks at the night sky through the cell window

- The religious views that the chaplain expresses are similar to those given by the *juge d'instruction* in the first chapter of the second part of the novel. At that point, Meursault listened passively, but now he counters them with his own ideas.
- The chapter charts an emotional journey on Meursault's part from despair to rage to happiness.
- Several of the ideas expressed in this chapter have parallels in Camus's philosophical writing, such as *Le Mythe de Sisyphe*.

Key quotations

Mais tout le monde sait que la vie ne vaut pas la peine d'être vécue. Dans le fond, je n'ignorais pas que mourir à trente ans ou à soixante-dix importe peu puisque, naturellement, dans les deux cas, d'autres hommes et d'autres femmes vivront, et cela pendant des milliers d'années.
(*Part II, Chapter 5*)

Si près de la mort, maman devait s'y sentir libérée et prête à tout revivre. Personne, personne n'avait le droit de pleurer sur elle. Et moi aussi, je me suis senti prêt à tout revivre.
(*Part II, Chapter 5*)

Quoting from the text can be a good way to support your argument with evidence. It shows you have a precise grasp of your material, and there is no clearer way to prove your point about the novel than by using the author's own words. Often only a short phrase, or sometimes even a single word, is all you need in order to back up your assertion.

 Activité 11

Contrairement à son caractère pendant le reste du roman, où Meursault se montre plutôt impassible, dans le dernier chapitre il ressent des émotions variées.

Trouvez une citation du dernier chapitre pour illustrer chacune de ces émotions éprouvées par Meursault :

1. l'espoir

2. l'irritation

3. la rage

4. le désespoir

5. la joie

6. la paix

Writing about plot

You will need to know the plot of *L'Étranger* in detail. Make sure that you understand the chain of events involving Raymond, Masson and the Arab characters that leads Meursault to the shooting. You will also need to be clear about the progression of the investigation, trial and sentence afterwards. Perhaps the trickiest part of the novel to get straight is the rather aimless and random life Meursault leads in much of the first half of the novel. It is worth spending time making sure you know how the funeral, work, home, beach and balcony scenes fit together, and in which order.

You are not familiarising yourself with the plot of the novel in order to be able to tell the story, however. In the exam, you should avoid lengthy summaries of the plot. Rather, you should use your knowledge to select precise examples of what happened in the story which can stand as evidence to prove the point you're making. These examples should be <u>accurate</u> and <u>concise</u> in your essay. Don't say more than you need in order to support your argument.

Structure

L'Étranger is divided into two parts. The first part of the novel takes place over around two weeks in summer. The second part spans a year, beginning just after Meursault's arrest, skimming rapidly over eleven months of prison, and ending with his trial and its aftermath the following summer.

The second half of the novel is very different from the first. The two halves of the story are divided by the shooting at the beach at the end of Part I, which will utterly change Meursault's life. So in the first half we have varied locations, in the second half only the prison and the courtroom. The first half is filled with activity: Meursault is a very physical person and always on the move. The second half shows him confined and still, and for the first time starting to think and explore his feelings and beliefs.

> ### Activité 12
>
> Faites une liste des huit lieux les plus importants du roman. Pouvez-vous associer à chacun un mot qui évoque l'humeur ou l'émotion suscitée chez Meursault par ce lieu?
>
> | 1. balcon | calme |
> | --- | --- |

The structure of the first part feels quite random, reflecting the aimlessness of Meursault's life. Weekdays and weekends at the office, beach or flat are recounted one after the other, without much **causal connection** between them. There is some development, such as the growing relationship between Meursault and Marie, or the building tension as Meursault becomes implicated in Raymond's wrongdoing, but, compared with many novels, there is little sense of a plot moving forward. This makes it all the more shocking when the events of the first half culminate in violent death.

The second half also contains a fair amount of aimless time in a prison cell, but there is now a terrible forward motion to the story, the 'rite implacable' *(Part II, Chapter 5)* of investigation, trial, sentence, appeal and execution.

Camus also uses the two-part structure of his novel to create narrative symmetry. There are many echoes in the second half of themes, characters and events in the first. The first and last chapter both refer to the cool of summer evenings as 'une trêve mélancolique' *(Part I, Chapter 1; Part II, Chapter 5)*. The punishing heat of the beach killing is echoed in the sweltering, airless courtroom, while the pleasant evening on the balcony is recalled in the brief moment between courtroom and prison van, where Meursault recognises 'l'odeur et la couleur du soir d'été' and 'les bruits familiers d'une ville que j'aimais' *(Part II, Chapter 3)*.

Almost everyone from the first half of the novel reappears in the second half, even the 'femme automate' *(Part II, Chapter 4)* Meursault once watched eat in Céleste's café. The other reappearing characters – the manager and concierge of the old people's home, Pérez, Céleste, Raymond, Masson, Salamano and Marie – return as witnesses in the trial. They are there specifically to retell the events of Part I of the novel, and to offer an interpretation of Meursault's behaviour and character during those events.

> **Key quotations**
>
> J'ai eu alors envie de fumer. Mais j'ai hésité parce que je ne savais pas si je pouvais le faire devant maman. J'ai réfléchi, cela n'avait aucune importance. J'ai offert une cigarette au concierge et nous avons fumé.
> *(Part I, Chapter 1)*
>
> Le vieux a dit d'un air embarrassé: « Je sais bien que j'ai eu tort. Mais je n'ai pas osé refuser la cigarette que monsieur m'a offerte. »
> *(Part II, Chapter 3)*

causal connection *le lien de causalité* a relationship between two events where one event causes the other

Activité 13

Faites une liste de tous les personnages secondaires qui deviennent témoins dans le procès de Meursault. Notez à quelle page du livre ils offrent leur témoignage et faites un court résumé de ce qu'ils disent.

Personnage	Page	Témoignage
Salamano	Part II, Ch. 3; p. 143	'j'avais été bon pour son chien'; 'je n'avais plus rien à dire à maman [...]'

Establishing a timeframe for the novel

Another curious thing about the narrative structure of *L'Étranger* is the question of <u>when</u> Meursault is telling his story. The novel is told in the **first person** and mostly in the past tense. Usually, when stories are told like this, they are narrated **retrospectively**, from a point after the end of the story. Less commonly, they can be narrated **intermittently**, from several different points within the time-span of the story. Novels told in the form of diaries are the most common examples of these, with each diary entry moving to a new time of narration, perhaps looking back on the events of the day from the evening.

first person *à la première personne* the story is told from the perspective of the main character, using the pronoun 'I' / *je*

retrospective narration *la narration rétrospective* the narrator is telling us the story looking back from a point in time after the end of the story has been reached

intermittent narration *la narration intermittente* the story is being told from a series of different points in time within the time-span of the story itself

Activité 14

1. Relisez cet extrait du premier chapitre du roman.

 Je prendrai l'autobus à 2 heures et j'arriverai dans l'après-midi. Ainsi, je pourrai veiller et je rentrerai demain soir. J'ai demandé deux jours de congé à mon patron et il ne pouvait pas me les refuser avec une excuse pareille. [...] Pour le moment, c'est un peu comme si maman n'était pas morte. Après l'enterrement, au contraire, ce sera une affaire classée et tout aura revêtu une allure plus officielle.

J'ai pris l'autobus à 2 heures. Il faisait très chaud.

(Part I, Chapter 1)

2. Soulignez tous les verbes dans le texte. Quel est le temps de chaque verbe?

3. Au commencement de l'extrait, quels événements sont dans le passé et lesquels dans l'avenir? À quel moment se situe le « maintenant » de la narration?

4. À la fin de l'extrait, quel changement s'est produit dans le temps de narration?

There are other points in the story where we can also see that the time of narration has changed. The very last chapter of the novel has a similar time-jump to the one in the first chapter that you can see in the activity box above. The opening lines of Part II, Chapter 5 seem to imply that Meursault has not yet met the prison chaplain as he is telling us the story. Then, later, the meeting with the chaplain is told in the past tense, meaning that the story is being told from a later point in time. Elsewhere in the story, Meursault makes scattered references to the time at which he's telling the story, like the **'aujourd'hui'** in the first line *(Part I, Chapter 1)* that shows us he's telling the story on the same day he received the telegram, or the **'hier c'était samedi'** and **'ce matin'** *(Part I, Chapter 4)* that suggest he's telling the story on a Sunday evening, a week after the funeral.

Key quotations

Aujourd'hui, maman est morte. *(Part I, Chapter 1; p. 9)*

Hier, c'était samedi, et Marie est venue [...]. Ce matin, Marie est restée. *(Part I, Chapter 4)*

Pour la troisième fois, j'ai refusé de recevoir l'aumônier. Je n'ai rien à lui dire, je n'ai pas envie de parler, je le verrai bien assez tôt. *(Part II, Chapter 5)*

C'est à ce moment précis que l'aumônier est entré. *(Part II, Chapter 5)*

The effect of this style of narration is subtle. Note that the time changes deliberately don't draw attention to themselves. You're not really supposed to notice them, unlike in a diary-form novel. But even if we don't notice it consciously, there are two important aspects of the way Meursault tells his story that affect the way we feel about it.

First, the way Meursault tells his story keeps us close to the action. He's telling his story from before, during, and very soon after the events he recounts. That's a good way of making the story seem vivid and immediate. Since so much of the story focuses on physical sensations, such as the brutal heat of the midday sun, putting us as readers so close to Meursault's experience as it happens helps us to share in this experience. It's almost as if we were there with him at the time.

Secondly, the fact that Meursault is telling his story before he's reached the end of it himself means that, as he tells it, he doesn't know where it's heading. So he tells us about his early entanglement with Raymond without knowing that it will lead to the shooting. He tells us innocently about what he did at the old people's home, unaware that his most trivial actions will later be used as evidence against him in a murder trial.

Contrast this with the way the story is retold during the trial by a hostile storyteller (the prosecutor) who knows exactly how it will end in violence. The prosecutor is determined to link every event in the story to this ending, either because it supposedly shows Meursault deliberately planning the killing, or because it betrays his cold, murderous character.

For Camus, too, intermittent narration suits the philosophy of life that underpins the story he is telling. **Existentialism** claims that there is no plan or purpose to our lives other than the ones we make for ourselves, and that life has neither a fixed goal nor a meaning. This method of telling a story through a storyteller who doesn't know what the ending will be, and who therefore doesn't know what his story will finally mean, fits better with Camus's view of life than a story told by a retrospective or **omniscient** narrator. The term 'omniscient' also has religious connotations, as being all-knowing is supposed to be an attribute of God. This may be another reason why Camus felt omniscient narration was not right for his novel.

existentialism *l'existentialisme (m)* a philosophy that humans are entirely free and must take responsibility for their own actions and choices, rejecting the idea that God or any force exists and can influence the future

omniscient *omniscient* 'knowing everything': an omniscient narrator is one who can tell us anything and everything about the characters and events of the story. Many novels have an omniscient narrator, including *Oliver Twist* by Charles Dickens and *The Lord of the Rings* by JRR Tolkien

Activité 15

1. Cherchez des exemples de narration rétrospective et de narration intermittente dans les romans (anglais ou français) que vous avez lus.

2. Connaissez-vous un roman à narration intermittente qui n'adopte pas la forme d'un journal intime?

3. Est-ce que le choix de narration a un effet sur l'histoire racontée ou sur l'expérience du lecteur?

4. Est-ce qu'un certain mode de narration convient à un genre particulier de roman (le roman policier, par exemple)?

5. Finalement, existe-t-il d'autres modes possibles de narration à part la narration rétrospective et la narration intermittente (une narration simultanée, par exemple, ou même une narration prospective)?

Writing about plot and structure

For the exam, you will need to know the plot and understand the structure of *L'Étranger* very well, so that you're able to draw on all parts of the novel for your answers. When writing essays on the novel, though, it's important that you don't drift into simply telling the story. Imagine that you are the prosecutor in a court case (like the public prosecutor in *L'Étranger*). You can't simply show the evidence to the jury and leave them to draw their own conclusions. You need to make a clear and persuasive case, and use the evidence to support it. In writing an essay, the plot of the novel, along with quotations and context, is your evidence, and your argument is your prosecution case. Make sure that it's always clear what the point you're making is, and how your reference to events in the novel supports that point. If your reader can't see why you've included something that happens in the novel, it shouldn't be in your essay.

You can also look at what happens in the novel from two perspectives: as a series of events in Meursault's life, and as elements of a work of literature artfully arranged by Camus. To grasp the former perspective, you need to make sure that you understand how events connect to one another, such as how the letter Meursault writes in Raymond's flat leads to the shooting on the beach. To grasp the second perspective, you need to look for symmetries and contrasts across the structure of the novel, such as how the deaths of Meursault's mother, the Arab man, and Meursault himself mark the beginning, middle and end of the story, or how the second chapter in both parts of the novel centres on sharply contrasting scenes between Meursault and Marie.

Vocabulary

abattre to shoot (down)

une affaire classée finished business

un asile care home

aura revêtu une allure will seem (literally, 'will have put on an appearance')

la balle bullet

le brassard (black) armband, worn as part of mourning dress

le congé leave (from work)

décédé dead, deceased

en deuil in mourning (dress)

un enterrement funeral, burial

étourdi confused, scatterbrained

la gâchette trigger

se pendre to hang oneself

posément coolly

le procès trial

le puits well

le témoin witness

le témoignage testimony, witness statement

valoir la peine to be worth the effort

veiller to watch over a coffin overnight

les vieillards (mpl) old people

le village natal the village where [he] was born

Useful phrases

Il y a un lien entre… There is a connection between…

…est un élément important de l'intrigue …is an important part of the plot

le développement de l'intrigue the unfolding of the plot

la structure symétrique du roman the novel's symmetrical structure

On voit le lien de causalité (entre)… We can see the causal link (between)…

Contrairement à ce qui se passe dans la première partie du roman… Unlike what happens in Part I of the novel…

Par contre, dans le prochain chapitre… In contrast, in the following chapter…

vers la fin du chapitre towards the end of the chapter

Le parallèle est évident entre… The parallel is clear between…

Le contraste est clair entre… The contrast is clear between…

Notons la ressemblance entre… Note the similarity between…

Comme nous le voyons au début / au milieu / au dénouement du roman… As we see at the beginning / middle / end of the novel…

l'intrigue progresse rapidement / lentement the plot develops quickly / slowly

un résumé de l'intrigue a plot summary

Author biography

- Camus was born in Algeria in 1913. His parents were poor French **colonists**. While Camus was still a baby, his parents moved from an Algerian village to the capital city, Algiers, shortly after which his father was killed fighting in the First World War.

- As a teenager, Camus played in goal for an Algerian youth football team. His sporting career was cut short when he developed tuberculosis at the age of 17. At around this time he discovered a passion for philosophy, and for politics. He joined the Algerian Communist Party in his early twenties.

- Camus worked as a journalist from the late 1930s. He was very critical of the impact of French colonialism on the poorest people in Algeria, although he stopped short of condemning the colonial project itself. He also spent some time in Paris working for the *Paris-Soir* newspaper. In *L'Étranger*, Meursault also mentions having worked in Paris.

Albert Camus

- In the early years of the Second World War, Camus was writing the two works with which he would make his name: the philosophical essay, *Le Mythe de Sisyphe* and the novel, *L'Étranger*. Both were published in 1942 and attracted the attention and praise of Jean-Paul Sartre, the influential philosopher, novelist and playwright.

- During the war, Camus became editor-in-chief of the Resistance newspaper, *Combat*.

- After the war, Camus published two further novels, *La Peste*, about a modern-day outbreak of bubonic plague, and *La Chute*, about a man who begins to question what sort of person he is after witnessing a suicide and failing to intervene. He also published a collection of short stories, *L'Exil et le Royaume*, several plays, essays and journalism.

- His work shares a philosophical outlook with Sartre in many respects, but he disliked being labelled together with the more famous writer as an 'existentialist'.

- In the 1950s, Sartre and Camus fell out over politics. Sartre strongly supported both the Russian Communist regime and Algerian calls for independence. Camus was not convinced by either.
- In the late 1950s, Camus was awarded the Nobel Prize for Literature and began work on a fourth novel, *Le Premier Homme*.
- In 1960, he was killed in a car crash with his publisher, Michel Gallimard, while travelling to Paris on icy roads. The unfinished manuscript for *Le Premier Homme* was found in the wreckage. He was 46 years old.

Activité 1

1. Faites des recherches sur Internet sur Albert Camus et Jean-Paul Sartre. Cherchez des informations sur

   a) leurs théories philosophiques et

   b) leurs opinions politiques.

2. Faites une liste de cinq points essentiels concernant la philosophie et / ou la politique de Sartre. Faites la même chose pour Camus.

3. Quelles étaient les similarités entre Sartre et Camus? Quelles étaient les différences?

Historical and cultural context

There are two main areas of context necessary for study to understand *L'Étranger* properly. The first is the historical setting of colonial Algeria, with its parallel communities of Arabs and ***pied-noir*** French colonists. The second is the novel's link to existentialist philosophy, and in particular the concept of **the Absurd**. This was important to Camus's novel and his essays, and to many writers and thinkers of the time.

black foot *le pied-noir* French slang term for white French settlers in Algeria during the colonial period, 1830–1962. Nobody really knows why the colonists were known as 'black feet'. One suggestion is that the term originally referred to the Algerian stokers who worked barefoot in the coal-heaps of steam-ships, then came to mean Algerians generally, and was then transferred to French people who had 'become' Algerian

colonist *le colon* a settler of a country that has been founded or conquered by the colonists' home country, or a member of a group descended from the original settlers (as is the case with Meursault)

the Absurd *l'Absurde (m)* in existentialist philosophy, a feeling of mismatch between the human desire to understand the meaning and purpose of everything, and the apparent lack of any meaning or purpose in the universe, seen from a non-religious perspective

Colonial Algeria

The colonial period in Algeria lasted from 1830, when invading French troops occupied the capital city, Algiers, until the country regained independence at the end of the Algerian War in 1962. Algeria was one of the largest, longest held, and most bitterly contested territories of France's colonial empire.

At its greatest extent in the early twentieth century, it encompassed large areas of North and West Africa and of South East Asia. At the time of *L'Étranger*, the total population of Algeria was around eight million people, of whom between 10 and 20% would have been European settlers.

The colonised Algerians were of Arab and Berber ethnicity (the French would often refer to them indiscriminately as 'Arabs') and almost all of them were Sunni Muslims. In Algiers, where the novel is set, white colonists would probably have made up the majority of the residents, and would have owned most of the wealth and property.

Colonial-era buildings in Algiers

The colonists were divided into the *grands colons*: wealthy landowners and businessmen who controlled most of Algeria's mining, agriculture and manufacturing, and the *petits colons*: individuals who had emigrated to Algeria with very little in search of a better life, and often remained in poverty. Camus's family belonged to this latter group.

While the lives of the *petits colons* often had more in common with those of the Muslim Algerians than with those of the rich *grands colons*, all the colonists had citizenship rights and political representation that was largely denied to the Arab and Berber people. Meursault seems far from wealthy, with his simple life living in his mother's old flat in a building with poor and disreputable neighbours, although he does have a 'white-collar' desk job, he has travelled to Europe, and he has disposable income to go to the cinema and eat out regularly at Céleste's restaurant.

At the time of the novel, all positions of authority, including everyone involved in Meursault's trial, would be held by white settlers. It would have been most unusual, perhaps even implausible, for a French colonist to be put on trial, found guilty and given the death penalty for killing an Arab. This may be one reason why the prosecution in the case largely ignores the killing itself, and instead focuses on Meursault's other behaviour to present a picture of him as morally degenerate.

Activité 2

Considérez le contexte colonial du roman. À votre avis, si Meursault avait tué un Blanc, est-ce qu'on lui aurait accordé le même traitement pendant son procès?

Vous pouvez utiliser les points suivants:

- La plupart des détenus que Meursault rencontre le jour de son arrestation sont des Arabes. Ils rient de voir un Blanc en prison.
- Le procureur néglige la victime arabe pour concentrer son attention sur l'interaction de Meursault avec d'autres Blancs.
- Le lecteur n'apprend jamais le nom des personnages arabes.

There was little social interaction between the two communities in this period. In the novel, Meursault has no Arab friends or acquaintances. The only relationship between a colonist and an Arab person that we see in *L'Étranger* is that between Raymond and his unnamed **mistress**, and that relationship barely deserves the name, revolving as it does around sex and money, and ending in violent physical abuse.

mistress *la maîtresse* unlike 'girlfriend', this suggests a woman in a relationship with a man that is more about sex than about love, and in which she has little power and may be financially dependent. It often refers to a woman in a sexual relationship with a married man, although this is not the case with Raymond. In Camus's day, it would be seen as a shameful situation for the woman in question

In 1954, 12 years after *L'Étranger* was published, Algerian unrest broke out into violence, and the war of independence began. Camus, who was by this time a well-known public intellectual and political activist, attempted to play a role in resolving the conflict, calling for an Algeria that would have a more equal footing with France, and have greater political rights for its Arab and Berber citizens, but would essentially remain a colony. In 1962, two years after Camus's death, Algeria won full independence from France.

Celebrations after the publication of the results of the 1962 Algerian independence referendum

Activité 3

a) Faites une chronologie de l'histoire de la colonisation de l'Algérie. Quels étaient les événements marquants à l'époque de la publication du roman de Camus? Selon vous, quels sont les événements les plus importants entre l'époque de *L'Étranger* et l'Algérie d'aujourd'hui?

b) En 2017, Emmanuel Macron, alors candidat à l'élection présidentielle, a qualifié la colonisation française de l'Algérie de « crime contre l'humanité », provoquant l'indignation de ses adversaires politiques. Faites quelques recherches sur Internet sur les débats provoqués par ses propos. Croyez-vous qu'il ait eu raison de s'exprimer ainsi?

Existentialism and the Absurd

Although Camus disliked being called an existentialist, the philosophical outlook on life that he expresses in *L'Étranger* has a lot in common with French existentialist thought, and with that of the movement's most famous thinker, Jean-Paul Sartre. On the key idea of the Absurd, a term which turns up frequently in their work, the two of them were closely in tune.

The starting point for existentialist thought is that there is no god, or at least not one who has any involvement in human affairs at the moment. This has two consequences. First, it means that there is no order or meaning in the universe. Everything in the world just happens to be there, rather than having been designed and placed by a creator, and everything that happens just happens, without being part of some divine plan. Secondly, it means that, where we're concerned as human beings, we have absolute freedom. There is no divine purpose in our lives, and no guidance from God about what is the right or wrong thing to do.

Existentialism suggests that with no higher power controlling us or telling us what to do, we have to decide on our own actions, and then be responsible for them afterwards. With great freedom, the existentialists argue, comes great responsibility.

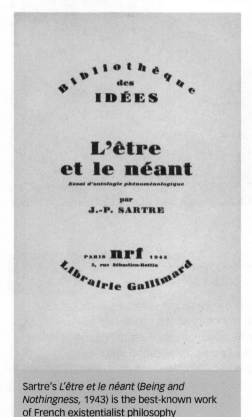

Sartre's *L'être et le néant* (*Being and Nothingness*, 1943) is the best-known work of French existentialist philosophy

In *Le Mythe de Sisyphe*, the philosophical essay he was writing at the same time as *L'Étranger*, Camus talks about what such a state of affairs might mean for how we experience the world and how we choose to live our lives. At the heart of the essay is the concept of the Absurd. Camus starts by discussing what the word 'absurd' means in everyday usage: a situation is absurd, he suggests, if it contains a mismatch of some kind. He offers the image of a man armed only with a knife attacking a machine-gunner: attacking with a knife is not absurd, nor is defending yourself with a machine gun. Only when the two are put together do things become absurd. The particular mismatch in the philosophical Absurd is between humans and the universe.

We like to understand things: we like things to have a purpose and a meaning, so that we can ask 'why?' and get a sensible answer. In the existentialist view, the universe has no answers for us, because it has no purpose and no meaning. This, according to Camus, makes our basic situation an absurd one. Meursault himself refers to his life as 'cette vie absurde' (*Part II, Chapter 5*) in the final pages of *L'Étranger*.

The central question of *Le Mythe de Sisyphe* is whether, in these circumstances, life is really worth living. Camus suggests we are all a little like Sisyphus in the Greek myth, condemned for all eternity pointlessly to roll a boulder up a hill, only to watch it roll back to the bottom, to begin the process again. Camus concludes that life is worth living, and what's more, that it is worth living with no illusions. He suggests we should boldly face up to our situation of living in a meaningless universe, with nothing but death waiting for us at the end, and nevertheless decide to make the best of things. He ends the essay with the famous line, 'Il faut imaginer Sisyphe heureux'.

Sisyphus, rolling his boulder up the hill

Using context in your writing

Knowing the context of the novel will help to make your answers more insightful. However, just as you are not being asked to tell the story of the novel, nor are you being asked to tell the story of Camus's life, or head into an account of Algerian history or existentialist philosophy. Rather, you need to use this background knowledge to enhance your answer to the exam question you are dealing with. Understanding the context of *L'Étranger* should help you focus on the question more precisely, not distract you from it.

Vocabulary

l'Absurde (m) the Absurd

Alger Algiers (capital city of Algeria)

l'Algérie (f) Algeria

l'Arabe (m/f) Arab (n)

arabe Arabic, Arab (adj)

athée atheist

l'authenticité (f) authenticity

le but purpose

le colon colonist

la colonisation colonisation

la conquête conquest

le crime contre l'humanité crime against humanity

dénoncer to denounce

l'indifférence (f) indifference

l'insurrection (f) revolt

la liberté freedom

la période coloniale colonial period

la philosophie philosophy

le pied-noir widespread term for Algerian colonists

religieux religious

la responsabilité responsibility

la sérénité serenity

la signification meaning

sans signification / dénué de sens meaningless

Useful phrases

Vu(e) dans le contexte de… Seen in the context of…

Il faut considérer le contexte de… We must consider the context of…

Le contexte historique / social / culturel du roman nous apprend que… the historical / social / cultural context of the novel tells us that…

En lisant le roman comme une œuvre de l'ère coloniale… Reading the novel as a work from the colonial era…

Une perspective philosophique nous montre que… A philosophical perspective shows us that…

la vision du monde exprimée dans le roman the world view expressed in the novel

…s'accorde avec la pensée existentialiste …is in line with existentialist thinking

une perspective religieuse, par contre a religious viewpoint, on the other hand

Un lecteur des années 1940 considérerait peut-être que… tandis qu'un lecteur d'aujourd'hui penserait peut-être que… A reader in the 1940s might consider that… whereas a present day reader might think that…

C'était un homme de son temps. He was a man of his time.

les attitudes contemporaines à ce sujet contemporary attitudes towards this subject

Main characters

Meursault

Meursault is the narrator and **protagonist** of the novel. He is a young man who works in an office in mid-twentieth-century Algiers under French colonisation. At the end of the novel, he makes a remark about dying 'à trente ans' *(Part II, Chapter 5)*, which, if it's a literal reference to his coming execution, would make him 29 at the start of the novel. He appears to have no family beyond the mother who dies at the start of the novel, and few friends or acquaintances beyond his neighbours and co-workers. He likes swimming and sunbathing, and watching the world go by from his balcony. Although he enters into a relationship with Marie, and even agrees to marry her, he says he does not love her and takes little interest in her life. Similarly, he was not close to his mother and did not visit her often after she moved to the old people's home. Although people seem to like him, he is a loner, and happy to be so. The novel's title, *L'Étranger*, is perhaps better translated as 'the outsider' rather than 'the stranger', as it suggests someone who does not fit in, staying at the margins of the community and out of step with other people.

> **protagonist** *le protagoniste* the central character in a story

Activité 1

Voici deux définitions du mot 'étranger':

1. qui n'a pas la nationalité du pays où il se trouve
2. qui ne fait pas partie d'un groupe, d'un milieu.

Dans quelle mesure ces définitions sont-elles applicables au personnage de Meursault? À votre avis, laquelle des deux est la plus importante dans le roman?

Before his arrest, Meursault has few likes or dislikes in his life. He notices physical sensations: cool seawater or evening air, which he likes, or damp towels at the office, which he doesn't. For most things his response is 'ça m'était égal' *(Part I, Chapter 3)*, meaning 'I had no opinion about it', or 'I didn't mind either way'. Where Meursault is unusual is that this is his response even to things we would really expect him to have an opinion about, including moral questions like whether Raymond is the kind of person he wants as a friend *(Part I, Chapter 3)*, and life-changing events like moving to Paris or getting married *(Part I, Chapter 5)*.

Meursault on his balcony, from *L'Étranger*, the graphic novel by Jacques Ferrandez. Ferrandez draws Meursault as a young man in his twenties, which is closer to Camus's conception of the character than the more middle-aged portrayal in the 1967 film

---

Key quotation

Le soir, Marie est venue me chercher et m'a demandé si je voulais me marier avec elle. J'ai dit que cela m'était égal et que nous pourrions le faire si elle le voulait.
(Part I, Chapter 5)

Meursault seems to feel few emotions beyond basic physical pleasures and discomforts. He feels no grief at his mother's death and does not cry at her funeral. Only towards the end of the story do his emotions begin to appear. Although he does not cry at the trial either, he does feel **'une envie stupide de pleurer'** *(Part II, Chapter 3)* as he realises how much he is hated by the people in the courtroom. It is only in the final scene in his prison cell that he could really be described as emotional, when the chaplain's offer to pray for him finally provokes a heartfelt reaction.

Key quotation

Alors, je ne sais pas pourquoi, il y a quelque chose qui a crevé en moi. Je me suis mis à crier à plein gosier et je l'ai insulté et je lui ai dit de ne pas prier. Je l'avais pris par le collet de sa soutane. Je déversais sur lui tout le fond de mon cœur avec des bondissements mêlés de joie et de colère.
(Part II, Chapter 5)

Activité 2

1. Meursault ne montre pas beaucoup d'émotion. Souvent, il ne paraît ni comprendre ni s'intéresser aux émotions des autres non plus. Relisez cette courte scène entre Meursault et Marie.

 J'ai raconté à Marie l'histoire du vieux et elle a ri. Elle avait un de mes pyjamas dont elle avait retroussé les manches. Quand elle a ri, j'ai eu encore envie d'elle. Un moment après, elle m'a demandé si je l'aimais. Je lui ai répondu que cela ne voulait rien dire, mais qu'il me semblait que non. Elle a eu l'air triste. Mais en préparant le déjeuner, et à propos de rien, elle a encore ri de telle façon que je l'ai embrassée.

(Part I, Chapter 4)

2. Comment expliquez-vous le comportement de Meursault? Considérez les quatre interprétations ci-dessous.

   a) Le comportement de Meursault envers Marie est cruel et grossier.

   b) Meursault démontre une insensibilité plutôt comique dans cette scène.

   c) L'honnêteté de Meursault dans cette scène est un trait admirable. Il refuse de mentir à Marie.

   d) Le comportement de Meursault ressemble à celui de quelqu'un atteint d'un trouble autistique.

   e) C'est la combinaison de ces quatre explications qui apporte l'interprétation la plus juste du comportement de Meursault.

   Êtes-vous d'accord avec une ou plusieurs? Justifiez votre réponse.

Meursault doesn't think deeply about moral issues, about the future, or about himself or other people. He writes the letter for Raymond because he can find no reason not to do so, even though the reader can probably find several. At the very least, Meursault is becoming embroiled in a scheme to brutally humiliate a young woman, and as things will turn out, he is also setting off a catastrophic series of events that will end in his own execution.

> **Key quotation**
>
> **J'ai fait la lettre. Je l'ai écrite un peu au hasard, mais je me suis appliqué à contenter Raymond parce que je n'avais pas de raison de ne pas le contenter.**
> *(Part I, Chapter 3)*

He is, though, extremely honest. He is honest in situations where the truth hurts other people, such as when his girlfriend asks if he loves her, and he is honest in situations where the truth is against his own interests. He tells the *juge d'instruction* that he is an atheist *(Part II, Chapter 1)*, and refuses to let his defence lawyer pretend that his lack of visible emotion at his mother's funeral was because he was hiding inner feelings. In both cases, a lie would have helped his chances of being found innocent, and since both are questions of his private feelings and beliefs, the lie would never have been found out.

> **Key quotation**
>
> Il m'a demandé s'il pouvait dire que ce jour-là j'avais dominé mes sentiments naturels. Je lui ai dit: « Non, parce que c'est faux. »
> *(Part II, Chapter 1)*

Activité 3

« Meursault: héros ou méchant? »

1. Cherchez dans le texte les qualités de Meursault, puis ses défauts.

2. D'après ce que vous avez trouvé, est-ce que Meursault est un héros ou un méchant?

Raymond

Raymond Sintès is Meursault's neighbour, and later his friend. He has links to organised crime *(le milieu)* and is believed by neighbours to be a pimp, living off the proceeds of prostituting women. He thinks that his mistress, an unnamed Arab woman, is cheating on him, and enlists Meursault in his plan to help 'punish' her. After Meursault has written the letter that lures the woman back to Raymond's flat, Raymond beats her brutally. Meursault testifies to the police on Raymond's behalf that the woman had been unfaithful, although he has only Raymond's word for this.

It is Raymond who invites Meursault to Masson's beach house, Raymond who provokes the brawl with the Arabs on the beach, and Raymond who brings the gun and considers using it before handing it to Meursault. Raymond is thus the instigator for much of what happens in the novel, and Meursault is often just passively compliant with his plans. He is violent and immoral, not only beating and humiliating his mistress, but later planning to shoot her brother in cold blood.

Activité 4

1. Relisez la conversation entre Raymond et Meursault dans le troisième chapitre du roman: « **Vous comprenez, monsieur Meursault, m'a-t-il dit, c'est pas que je suis méchant, mais je suis vif. [...]** » C'était aussi mon avis. *(Part I, Chapter 3)*

2. Examinez en détail les paroles de Raymond que Meursault cite directement, et celles qu'il paraphrase dans son récit.

3. Comment décririez-vous la façon de parler de Raymond? Cherchez des exemples de mots ou de phrases qui sont révélateurs de la personnalité de Raymond et de son attitude envers sa maîtresse et le frère de celle-ci.

During the trial, Raymond does try to show some loyalty and responsibility as he clumsily speaks up for Meursault, but his insistence that the shooting was down to chance does little to help Meursault's case, once the prosecutor raises Meursault's involvement in every link of the chain of events that led to it.

> **Key quotation**
>
> Raymond m'a demandé: « **Je le descends?** » J'ai pensé que si je disais non il s'exciterait tout seul et tirerait certainement. Je lui ai seulement dit: « **Il ne t'a pas encore parlé. Ça ferait vilain de tirer comme ça.** »
> *(Part II, Chapter 6)*

Activité 5

Si on considère ses actions, est-ce qu'il est possible d'avoir de la sympathie pour Raymond? Justifiez votre réponse.

Raymond's personality allows his character to serve as a **foil** to Meursault's. Both men are of similar age and background, and find themselves in similar situations. That enables us to compare their very different attitudes and behaviour, and see Meursault more clearly in the comparison.

> **foil** *le faire-valoir* a character who contrasts with another character in a story (usually the protagonist) in order to highlight the qualities of this second character. Dr Watson is a foil to Sherlock Holmes, as Watson's simplicity highlights Holmes's intelligence. Draco Malfoy is a foil to Harry Potter, as his meanness and cowardice highlight Harry's goodness and bravery

Activité 6

Comparez Raymond et Meursault. Quelles différences trouvez-vous entre les deux hommes? Y a-t-il aussi quelques similarités?

Marie

Meursault tells us Marie Cardona is a former typist from his office 'dont j'avais envie à l'époque' *(Part I, Chapter 2)*. They meet by chance swimming at the beach on the morning after Meursault's mother's funeral, and their relationship begins almost immediately, and with a strongly sexual element. Meursault brushes against her breasts as he helps her onto a buoy, then rests his head on her stomach as they sunbathe. He invites her to the cinema that evening, where they fondle and kiss, after which Marie spends the night in his bed.

Meursault and Marie on the beach in Visconti's film adaptation

Meursault's interest in Marie seems mostly sexual, and since in the novel we are seeing everything through his eyes, there is a lot of focus on Marie's body and her attractiveness.

> **Key quotation**
>
> Hier, c'était samedi et Marie est venue, comme nous en étions convenus. J'ai eu très envie d'elle parce qu'elle avait une belle robe à raies rouges et blanches et des sandales de cuir. On devinait ses seins durs et le brun du soleil lui faisait un visage de fleur.
> *(Part I, Chapter 4)*

After his arrest, Meursault sees Marie for a single visit in the prison visiting room, and then not at all. She tells him in a letter that she has been forbidden to visit as they are not married. Meursault says that his darkest times began after receiving that letter *(Part II, Chapter 2)*. It is not clear whether his depression is triggered by losing Marie as a person, or whether it is more what she has come to represent for him: female beauty, sexual relationships, and a last link to his old life before the shooting. Shortly afterwards, Meursault himself says: 'Je ne pensais jamais à Marie particulièrement. Mais je pensais tellement à une femme, aux femmes [...]' *(Part II, Chapter 2)*.

Because Meursault as a storyteller has little interest in Marie beyond the physical, we do not actually learn very much about her life or her character. She herself raises the issue shortly after they have decided to get married. He suggests dinner at Céleste's restaurant and she turns him down, saying she has 'things to do'. When he fails to ask her about them, she demands **'Tu ne veux pas savoir ce que j'ai à faire?'** *(Part I, Chapter 5)*, and laughs at his confusion as he admits it hadn't occurred to him to ask.

We do discover some of her similarities and differences from Meursault. Like him, she is young and lively, enjoying independent life and the pleasures of beach life and sexual relationships. Unlike him, she is always laughing, something which attracts the quiet protagonist to her. She also considers his behaviour sometimes inappropriate: when she sees his black tie after they get changed at the beach and learns of his mother's funeral the day before, she reacts negatively: **'elle a eu un petit recul, mais n'a fait aucune remarque'** *(Part I, Chapter 2)*. However, unlike the people we meet in the second half of the novel, she is tolerant of his eccentricity. It may even be part of her attraction to him.

Key quotation

Elle a murmuré que j'étais bizarre, qu'elle m'aimait sans doute à cause de cela mais que peut-être un jour je la dégoûterais pour les mêmes raisons. *(Part I, Chapter 5)*

Activité 7

Construisez un schéma en toile d'araignée, en français ou en anglais, sur les activités et les conversations de Meursault et Marie. Pour chaque activité ou conversation, expliquez comment elle éclaire les deux personnages et leurs relations.

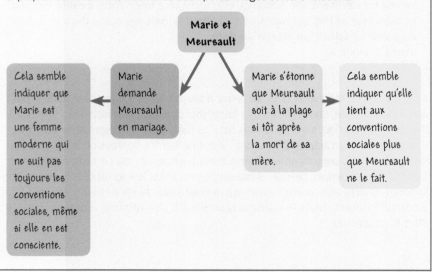

Writing about characters

Be precise and as detailed as possible when you discuss the characters. Make sure you know how to spell their names correctly. 'Meursault', in particular, is an easy name to misspell! It can be useful to keep a file on the basic details the novel tells us about each of the characters, for example:

Full name of character	Age	Job	Appearance	Personality	Relationship to Meursault	Trial witness?
Marie Cardona	Young (20s?)	Former typist at Meursault's office	Tanned skin, pretty and slim	Cheerful: often laughing Self-confident: proposes marriage	Work colleague, girlfriend, then fiancée	Yes (recounts day after funeral)
Raymond Sintès						

Minor characters

Activité 8

Choisissez un des personnages mineurs du roman. (Choisissez entre Salamano, Céleste, Monsieur Pérez, Masson, le juge d'instruction, le procureur, l'aumônier, l'Arabe, l'avocat de Meursault, la maîtresse de Raymond et la mère de Meursault.) Que savons-nous de cette personne? Quelle est son importance dans la vie de Meursault? Quelle est son importance pour l'intrigue ou pour les thèmes du roman de Camus?

Salamano

Salamano is Meursault's elderly neighbour, a widower who has lived alone with a spaniel for the last eight years. Both Salamano and the dog suffer from a disease that leaves their skin crusted with scabs. Salamano beats, drags and swears at the dog, which is terrified of him. On Salamano's second appearance in the novel, he has lost the dog, which slipped its collar while Salamano was distracted at a fair. He is upset at the loss, but rages at the thought of paying a fee to the dog-pound to get the animal back. That night, Meursault hears Salamano crying. The last time Meursault sees Salamano before his trial, he is nostalgic about the dog, and admits how much it meant to him.

Activité 9

Son lit a craqué. Et au bizarre petit bruit qui a traversé la cloison, j'ai compris qu'il pleurait. Je ne sais pas pourquoi j'ai pensé à maman.

(Part I, Chapter 4)

À votre avis, pourquoi est-ce que le bruit des larmes de Salamano fait penser Meursault à sa mère? Pourquoi ne comprend-il pas lui-même la raison?

Activité 10

Imaginez une version du roman dans laquelle on aurait supprimé toute mention de Salamano et de son chien. Est-ce que le lecteur en remarquerait l'absence? Dans quelle mesure le roman serait-il différent?

Céleste

Céleste runs a restaurant at which Meursault often eats. Céleste also considers himself a friend of Meursault. At the trial, he tries to speak up for Meursault, but is very inarticulate.

Monsieur Pérez

Thomas Pérez is known jokingly at the old people's home as Meursault's mother's 'fiancé'. On the day of the burial, he struggles to keep up with the funeral procession and faints at the grave-side. His grief is contrasted with Meursault's lack of emotion by the prosecutor during the trial. Meursault thinks of him again in the novel's final pages, and sees his mother's decision to start a relationship with him as a sign of her wish to live life fully, even in older age.

Activité 11

Comparez et commentez le comportement de Meursault et de Thomas Pérez à l'enterrement de la mère de Meursault et pendant les heures qui le précèdent. Pour lequel des deux hommes ressentez-vous le plus de sympathie? Justifiez votre réponse.

Masson

Masson is a friend of Raymond's. He and his wife own the beach house to which Raymond invites Meursault and Marie on the day of the killing. Masson participates in the beach brawl with the Arabs. Later, he gives evidence in support of Meursault in the trial, but, like Meursault's other defenders, he has little of substance to say and fails to help his cause.

Meursault, Masson and Raymond, from Jacques Ferrandez's graphic novel of *L'Étranger*

Le juge d'instruction

Unlike British and American criminal proceedings, French legal cases are led by an examining magistrate *(juge d'instruction)*, who is involved in the case from an early stage, and whose task it is to call witnesses, appoint a prosecutor, and decide which evidence is admissible for the trial. In *L'Étranger*, Meursault meets the *juge d'instruction* regularly for questioning during the year between his arrest and his trial. Note that the *juge d'instruction* does not preside over the trial itself. There are three judges in the courtroom at Meursault's trial, the most important of whom is referred to as *le président*. He is not the same person as the *juge d'instruction*. At their first meeting, the *juge d'instruction* becomes enraged by Meursault's inability to explain his actions on the beach, and by his admission that he does not believe in God. He waves a crucifix in Meursault's face and demands that he have faith. Over the months that follow, they develop a friendly relationship, and the *juge d'instruction* refers to him jokingly as 'monsieur l'Antéchrist' *(Part II, Chapter 1)*.

The prosecutor

The public prosecutor (*le procureur*) examines the witnesses during the trial, and builds the case for a guilty verdict. We see in his questioning of the witnesses and his summing-up speech to the jury that his aim is to get a conviction by:

- demonstrating from the events immediately before the killing that the crime was premeditated (planned)
- showing that Meursault is an evil person by using evidence from elsewhere in his life, most particularly from his behaviour during and after his mother's funeral.

The prosecutor uses complex, emotive and persuasive language, embellishing the facts to show Meursault in as bleak a light as possible. He is theatrical, shouting out in triumph and anger. He pretends not to know, then not to care, about the date Marie began her relationship with Meursault, then traps her into portraying his behaviour on the day after the funeral as heartless *(Part II, Chapter 3)*. He exaggerates to emphasise his point, claiming, for example, that Meursault 'n'en avai[t] point, d'âme, et que rien d'humain, et pas un des principes moraux qui gardent le cœur des hommes ne [lui] était accessible' *(Part II, Chapter 4)*. He often seems ridiculous in the novel as he ignores the shooting itself to build his case around Meursault drinking coffee at the old people's home or seeing a comedy film. Meursault is confused and his lawyer frustrated by the apparent irrelevance of the evidence he focuses on. However, it soon becomes clear that his approach has been devastatingly effective in persuading the jury and the judges that Meursault deserves the harshest punishment.

Courtroom scene from Visconti's 1967 film adaptation

The chaplain

The prison chaplain (*l'aumônier*) appears only in the final chapter of the book, and plays a similar role in the story to the *juge d'instruction*, in that he criticises Meursault's world view and urges him to have faith in God. Unlike with the *juge d'instruction*, Meursault counter-attacks with a passionate defence of his own belief in a Godless universe with no hope of salvation or afterlife, and a single life to live before the finality of death. The chaplain is intimidated by Meursault's violent words in much the same way that Meursault was intimidated by the *juge d'instruction*'s religious ranting, creating a symmetry between the first and last scenes of the novel's second half.

The Arab man

The Arab man (*l'Arabe*) whom Meursault shoots on the beach is the brother of Raymond's mistress. We first hear of him when Raymond explains to Meursault why his hand is injured. After Raymond had accused his mistress of cheating on him and beaten her until she bled, the brother confronted him on a bus and challenged him to a fight. They got off the bus together, Raymond hit first, and continued to kick the Arab man as he lay on the ground. After Raymond's 'revenge' on his mistress, he tells Meursault over the phone that the brother and other Arab men have been following him. As Raymond and Meursault leave for Masson's beach house, they are watched by a group of Arabs, two of whom follow them to the beach, including the brother. There are three encounters at the beach: a brawl between all five men, during which the brother uses a knife; a stand-off at the rocks, where Meursault dissuades Raymond from shooting the brother and takes his gun off him; and the final encounter, where Meursault is dazzled by the sun on the Arab man's knife, shoots him dead, and shoots four more bullets into his body.

Activité 12

L'Arabe est-il un personnage important ou un personnage secondaire dans le roman? Pourrait-on même dire que ce n'est pas du tout un personnage à proprement parler?

1. Faites une liste des raisons pour et contre.

2. À l'aide de votre liste, décidez si l'Arabe est un personnage important dans le roman. Justifiez votre décision.

Important	Sans importance
Scène avec Meursault au milieu du livre	Il ne dit rien (sauf dans le récit de Raymond)

If the Arab man is not a major character in the novel, is he really just a **plot device**? In his preface to *L'Étranger* for an American University Edition of the novel, Camus summed up the story as follows.

> **Key quotation**
>
> Dans notre société tout homme qui ne pleure pas à l'enterrement de sa mère risque d'être condamné à mort. (*Préface à l'édition universitaire américaine*)

If that's what the novel is about, then perhaps Camus just needed something – anything – that Meursault could be put on trial for, so that the trial could then focus on his behaviour at the funeral and the other ways in which he doesn't 'play the game' or behave like other people in society. He chose the shooting of an Arab man, ambiguously presented between accidental and deliberate, as the event for the courtroom to ignore, but that doesn't make the novel about that Arab man and his death.

plot device *le procédé narratif* an event or character designed to enable a plot development in the story

Meursault's lawyer

Meursault's defence lawyer (*l'avocat*) appears in the second half of the novel. He discusses the case with Meursault in the first chapter, then questions witnesses, objects to the prosecutor's approach, and sums up the case during the trial. In his interview with Meursault, he tries to persuade his client to put a positive 'spin' on his account of his behaviour, but Meursault refuses. In the trial, he struggles to keep proceedings focused on the facts of the shooting, and his appeals to reason are outclassed by the prosecutor's emotive speeches.

Raymond's mistress

Raymond's mistress (*maîtresse*) is an Arab woman, sister of the man Meursault will later kill. According to Raymond, he pays her rent and gives her a small allowance to live on. He claims he expects her to be faithful to him, but suspects she has been cheating on him after discovering that she has taken two bracelets to the pawnbroker's (bracelets which he assumes were given to her by another lover). He beats her **'jusqu'au sang'** *(Part I, Chapter 3)*. Some days later, she is lured to Raymond's flat by the letter Meursault has written, where Raymond has sex with her, then spits in her face and beats her again. (Meursault and Marie hear the assault through the wall.) We see her very briefly in the hallway outside the flat, where, in her only line of the novel, she tells a policeman « **Il m'a tapée. C'est un maquereau** » *(Part I, Chapter 4)*. Her accusation that Raymond is 'un maquereau' (a pimp) is repeated by other characters in the novel. It raises the possibility that the mistress is one of the women he is prostituting and that the dispute about the bracelets is not in fact caused by his jealousy, but by her status as a sex-worker who must give a percentage of her earnings to Raymond, and by his suspicion that she has a lover or client whom she is keeping secret from him.

Meursault's mother

Meursault's mother dies before the story begins, but she has a significant presence in the novel. She had no other family than Meursault, and until her move to the old people's home three years earlier, she and Meursault lived together, during which period she would spend her time **'à me suivre des yeux en silence'** *(Part I, Chapter 1)*. At the retirement home she seems to have found a new lease of life in her final years, even taking herself a 'fiancé' in the shape of M. Pérez.

Activité 13

« Bien qu'elle soit morte avant le commencement du récit, la mère de Meursault joue néanmoins un rôle très important dans l'histoire. » Êtes-vous d'accord avec cette déclaration? Justifiez votre réponse.

The trial judge

The trial judge (*le président*) is the leader of the three judges who preside over Meursault's trial. He gives the death sentence to Meursault after the jury has found him guilty.

The manager and concierge of the old people's home

The manager (*le directeur*) and concierge (*le concierge*) of the old people's home are the two people Meursault talks to when he goes to the home for his mother's funeral. A concierge has a role somewhere between caretaker, doorman and receptionist. The concierge gives Meursault a coffee and accepts a cigarette from him during the watch over the coffin. Both the manager and concierge are called as witnesses in the trial, where they talk about Mme Meursault's complaints about her son when she was alive, and his casual behaviour and lack of visible grief at her funeral.

Meursault sits by his mother's coffin in Visconti's film adaptation

Emmanuel

Emmanuel is Meursault's co-worker in the office. They have a friendly relationship. Meursault borrows a black tie for the funeral from Emmanuel, and in Part I, Chapter 3 we see them laughing together after jumping on a moving truck to hitch a ride. Emmanuel and Meursault's boss are the only people Meursault interacts with in the first part of the novel who do not reappear as trial witnesses in the second part.

Characters, plot, and themes

It can be helpful to think separately about the characters, plot, and themes of the novel in order to explore each aspect of it in a systematic way. It's also a good exercise, though, to explore how each one interacts with the other two. The American novelist Henry James once wrote:

> What is character but the determination of incident? What is incident but the illustration of character?
>
> *(The Art of Fiction)*

In other words, James is saying that the point of characters is to drive the plot through their particular attitudes and behaviour, and the point of plot is to highlight characters through the ways they act and react. Each is in the service of the other, and they can't be fully disentangled.

In *L'Étranger*, we might say that Meursault's character trait of absolute honesty is essential to the plot, as his refusal to feign grief or remorse is part of the reason he is condemned to death. At the same time, the plot of the trial and verdict serves to emphasise this trait of his personality. We could also say that the theme of morality or honesty is essential to both plot and character in the novel, and that both plot and character serve to illustrate this theme.

Consider whether there are any other characters, themes or plot developments from the novel that are dependent on each other. Explore these in your revision to help you understand the connections which can be made between these fundamental elements of the novel.

Activité 14

Examinez le schéma en toile d'araignée à la page 50. Composez deux phrases pour chaque personnage pour éclairer **a)** leur caractère et **b)** leur rôle dans l'histoire.

Par exemple:
L'avocat de Meursault est bien intentionné mais inefficace.
Il fait de son mieux pour que le procès se concentre sur ce qui s'est effectivement passé à la plage, mais il n'y parvient pas.

Character map

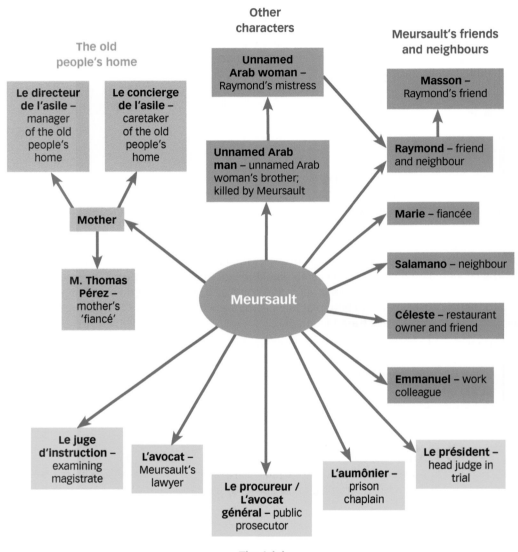

Other characters

The old people's home

Meursault's friends and neighbours

Le directeur de l'asile – manager of the old people's home

Le concierge de l'asile – caretaker of the old people's home

Unnamed Arab woman – Raymond's mistress

Unnamed Arab man – unnamed Arab woman's brother; killed by Meursault

Masson – Raymond's friend

Raymond – friend and neighbour

Marie – fiancée

Salamano – neighbour

Céleste – restaurant owner and friend

Emmanuel – work colleague

Mother

M. Thomas Pérez – mother's 'fiancé'

Meursault

Le juge d'instruction – examining magistrate

L'avocat – Meursault's lawyer

Le procureur / L'avocat général – public prosecutor

L'aumônier – prison chaplain

Le président – head judge in trial

The trial

Vocabulary

accommodant / facile à vivre easy-going

agressif aggressive

l'aumônier (m) chaplain

le bondissement surge, leap

le caractère personality

la cloison (internal) wall, partition

craquer to creak

crever to burst

la dactylo typist

l'employé (m) de bureau office worker

l'humeur (f) mood

le maquereau pimp

le milieu the 'mob', organised crime

le personnage character (in a story)

à plein gosier full-throated

profiter de la vie enjoy life

la raie stripe

le solitaire loner

la soutane cassock

Legal roles:

l'avocat (m) lawyer (in the novel, usually refers to Meursault's defence lawyer)

l'huissier (m) bailiff

le juge judge

le juge d'instruction examining magistrate

le juré juror

le président presiding judge

le procureur (also called *l'avocat général*) public prosecutor

le témoin witness

Useful phrases

Ce contraste entre Raymond et Meursault illustre… This contrast between Raymond and Meursault illustrates…

c'est un personnage passif / décontracté he's a passive / an easygoing character

il a un caractère violent / brutal he has a violent / abusive personality

On peut la caractériser comme… She can be characterised as…

L'avocat général / Le procureur le dépeint comme… The prosecutor describes him as…

Le personnage sert de faire-valoir pour… The character serves as a foil for / to…

Ses actions nous montrent que… His / Her actions show us that…

Si on l'examine de plus près… If we examine him more closely…

le juger par ses actes / par ses paroles to judge him by his actions / by his words

le considérer d'un point de vue moral to consider him from a moral point of view

l'évaluer d'une perspective psychologique to evaluate him / her from a psychological perspective

Ce personnage joue un rôle essentiel dans… This character plays a vital role in…

Meursault as narrator

What is most striking about the language Camus uses to tell his story is its simplicity.

- Camus mostly uses the perfect tense (*passé composé*) instead of the past historic (*passé simple*) more normally used in novels. While there's no real difference in meaning, the perfect is associated with speech and the past historic with writing. This means that Meursault's story feels almost like he's telling it to us directly. It feels less crafted as a piece of formal literary writing and more spontaneous.

- The vocabulary used is mostly fairly simple. Meursault rarely uses long or obscure words.

- He describes things in plain and straightforward terms. There are few adjectives or adverbs, and no long descriptive passages.

- Sentences are often short.

- Where sentences are longer, clauses are often linked with a simple 'et' or 'mais', rather than a more complex conjunction.

- Meursault's language is sometimes repetitive, as with his frequent refrain, 'ça m'était égal'.

The language used by Meursault engages the reader directly in his story

Activité 1

Analysez cet extrait du roman. Combien des caractéristiques dans la liste à la page 52 pouvez-vous trouver? Peut-on mieux comprendre le caractère de Meursault à travers sa façon de s'exprimer? Est-ce que l'effet de ce style est réussi, à votre avis?

> Nous sommes montés et j'allais le quitter quand il m'a dit: « J'ai chez moi du boudin et du vin. Si vous voulez manger un morceau avec moi?... » J'ai pensé que cela m'éviterait de faire ma cuisine et j'ai accepté. Lui aussi n'a qu'une chambre, avec une cuisine sans fenêtre. Au-dessus de son lit, il a un ange en stuc blanc et rose, des photos de champions et deux ou trois clichés de femmes nues. La chambre était sale et le lit défait. Il a d'abord allumé sa lampe à pétrole, puis il a sorti un pansement assez douteux de sa poche et a enveloppé sa main droite. Je lui ai demandé ce qu'il avait. Il m'a dit qu'il avait eu une bagarre avec un type qui lui cherchait des histoires.

(Part I, Chapter 3)

Camus's other novels and essays demonstrate that he has a wide vocabulary and a sophisticated prose style. For *La Chute*, in fact, Camus invents a narrator who is very keen on flowery expressions and complex grammar, the exact opposite of Meursault. So the choice of style for *L'Étranger* must be for a reason, and that reason must be to do with the sort of person Meursault is, and the approach to life that he holds.

What is it about Meursault that makes him talk like this? Well, first, he is not a natural storyteller. He seems to be of average intelligence, with an average-sized vocabulary and the ability to construct sentences that are grammatically correct, but not necessarily complex or eloquent. As a character in his own story he says relatively little – until his long speech at the end, that is – and what he does say is expressed in simple terms.

Key quotation

Sur la plage, je me suis étendu à plat ventre près de Masson et j'ai mis ma figure dans le sable. Je lui ai dit que « c'était bon » et il était de cet avis. *(Part I, Chapter 6)*

He seems not to be especially creative or imaginative. He displays little curiosity, and is not inclined to analyse his experience, or other people's.

Key quotation

Elle s'est demandé alors si elle m'aimait et moi, je ne pouvais rien savoir sur ce point. *(Part I, Chapter 5)*

This attitude might even be reflected in the grammar Camus has chosen to use. If there are not many conjunctions like 'parce que', 'car', 'bien que' or 'puisque' in the story, it's because sentences containing them are about <u>why</u> something has happened. Meursault rarely asks the question, and so rarely needs to use them. Instead, the **syntax** he uses is very suitable for someone who just takes life as it comes. One thing happens after another, and Meursault tells it to us plainly, without pausing to delve any deeper into the reasons behind his or other people's behaviour.

Language and character

Meursault's voice, though, is not the only one we hear in the novel. In later chapters we also hear the voices of other people at the trial. Among these is the prosecutor, whom Meursault quotes at slightly implausible length and detail. It's very important for the novel that he does this, however, as it allows Camus to retell the novel's first half, but this time using radically different language and style.

Activité 2

1. Relisez cet exemple typique de **la rhétorique** du procureur.

« […] Mais quand il s'agit de cette cour, la vertu toute négative de la tolérance doit se muer en celle, moins facile, mais plus élevée, de la justice. Surtout lorsque le vide du cœur tel qu'on le découvre chez cet homme devient un gouffre où la société peut succomber. »

(Part II, Chapter 4)

2. Analysez l'extrait. Quelles techniques le procureur utilise-t-il pour impressionner et persuader ses auditeurs? Cherchez des exemples des éléments suivants.

   a) métaphore

   b) **hyperbole** / exagération

   c) noms abstraits

   d) vocabulaire sophistiqué

   e) expressions rhétoriques

   f) appels à l'émotion

syntax *la syntaxe* the arrangement of words and phrases to create sentences
rhetoric *la rhétorique* persuasive use of language, especially through finely crafted or emotive expressions
hyperbole *l'hyperbole (f)* the use of exaggeration to create a strong impression

Activité 3

1. Le procureur résume les événements de la première partie du roman en représentant Meursault comme un méchant qui a prémédité son crime. Relisez l'extrait ci-dessous.

 « Le même homme qui au lendemain de la mort de sa mère se livrait à la débauche la plus honteuse a tué pour des raisons futiles et pour liquider une affaire de mœurs inqualifiable. »

(Part II, Chapter 3)

2. Imaginez que vous êtes l'avocat de Meursault. Composez un résumé avec un point de vue différent, selon lequel Meursault est présenté comme un homme de bonne volonté et la mort de l'Arabe comme accidentelle.

Other characters have a particular manner of speaking which helps to differentiate them and make them more memorable, such as Masson's verbal tic of saying, **'et je dirai plus'**, e.g. *Part I, Chapter 6*. Sometimes this way of talking helps illustrate the character. Raymond, for instance, talks brutally to Meursault about his mistress, using crude or violent terms like **'son coït'** or **'la « marquer »'** (that is, disfigure her) in *Part 1, Chapter 3*.

Be aware that the relationship between language and character is not always a straightforward one, however. The most vicious language used in the novel is the language Salamano uses towards his dog: **« Salaud! Charogne! »** *(Part I, Chapter 3)*. Only when the dog is gone do we discover that these hateful words masked a real affection towards the dog on Salamano's part.

Salamano uses cruel language, yet is heartbroken when his dog runs away

Metaphor and symbolism

Metaphors and **symbols** are literary devices that have a secondary meaning beyond their literal meaning. A 'new dawn' in a story might be a literal sunrise, but also a metaphor for a fresh start in a character's life, for instance. We use metaphors all the time when we are using non-literal expressions, often without even realising it. If you describe someone running fast as 'flying along', and someone walking slowly as 'at a crawl', then both your descriptions are metaphorical. When Meursault talks of Marie as having 'un visage de fleur' *(Part I, Chapter 4)*, he is using metaphor.

Symbols are related to metaphors. Indeed, the terms 'symbolic' and 'metaphorical' can sometimes be used interchangeably. While almost any non-literal use of language can be a metaphor, however, the term 'symbol' is usually reserved for non-literal meanings which are important to the themes of the story. It also is generally used to refer to something which exists in the world of the story, while a metaphor can simply be a turn of phrase.

> **metaphor** *la métaphore* a word or phrase being used to represent or suggest something other than its literal meaning, e.g. the heart as a metaphor for love
>
> **symbol** *le symbole* something in a work of literature that stands for or represents something else, often a material object, and usually representing an important theme in the story

A symbol might be a material object, such as Meursault's balcony above the street, which could be seen to symbolise his detachment from the community. (The literal distance between him and the young people in the street below could be read figuratively to represent how far removed he feels from everyday society.) A symbol doesn't always have to be a thing, however: you could suggest that the activity of swimming symbolises freedom in the novel.

Meursault is down-to-earth and plain-speaking. He uses comparatively little metaphorical language in his storytelling, and he does not seem aware of the symbolic overtones with which Camus invests some of the things around him. There is one point in the story, however, where he turns extensively to metaphor in order to express himself. That point is the shooting on the beach and the moments leading up to it. You can explore it in Activity 4.

Swimming in the ocean symbolises freedom for Meursault

 Activité 4

D'habitude, Meursault s'exprime dans un style simple et clair pour raconter son histoire, par exemple:

 Aujourd'hui j'ai beaucoup travaillé au bureau. Le patron a été aimable.

(Part I, Chapter 3)

Cependant, la dernière scène sur la plage est racontée dans un style plus soutenu, en utilisant plusieurs images et métaphores, par exemple:

- un océan de métal bouillant
- une longue lame étincelante qui m'atteignait au front
- ce rideau de larmes et de sel

- les cymbales du soleil
- cette épée brûlante
- pleuvoir du feu
- la porte du malheur

(Part I, Chapter 6)

1. Choisissez une de ces sept images. Qu'est-ce que Meursault décrit à travers la métaphore? Pourquoi Meursault a-t-il choisi cette image?

2. Regardez toutes les métaphores. Voyez-vous des liens entre les différentes images? Pourquoi y a-t-il tant de métaphores à ce moment de l'histoire?

Metaphor and symbolism

Look for metaphors and symbols in the text. If what is happening at a particular moment in the story seems to have a wider link to other themes of the novel, you may be able to interpret it metaphorically. Visual images created in the story may also stand as metaphors or be given symbolic meaning. So Meursault's balcony above the busy street may symbolise his outsider status; swimming in the sea may represent freedom.

Language nuance

Lastly, **nuance**: the smallest choices of language can sometimes be worth our attention, like the choice of a particular verb. Meursault's guilt or innocence hangs on the question of <u>why</u> he pulled the trigger on the beach. Was it an accident, or premeditated murder? If you look at the actual moment of the shooting, you will notice that Meursault does not say he pulled the trigger, which would be 'j'ai appuyé sur la gâchette'. Instead, he uses a different phrasing, **'la gâchette a cédé'** *(Part I, Chapter 6)*, which makes the trigger the subject of the verb rather than himself. The choice of construction highlights what was done and omits to say who did it. Expressing himself in this way might be an attempt to avoid taking responsibility for an action, or perhaps to suggest that the action was not deliberate. Meursault's simple honesty suggests the latter is more likely.

> **nuance** *la nuance* subtle differences, or shades of meaning in a writer's choice of vocabulary

Writing about language

Examining the kind of language with which a story is being told is always a useful way to understand what kind of story it is. In *L'Étranger*, it is absolutely vital, since our storyteller is also our protagonist, and the way Meursault expresses himself is closely connected to the sort of person he is. You might want to memorise a few examples of sentences that illustrate his personality through his storytelling style.

It's also worth focusing on the re-telling of events by the witnesses and prosecutor in the second half of the novel, and perhaps also memorising one or two pairs of sentences recounting the same thing from different perspectives. Look too at the way characters use language, and if it illustrates the kind of people they are.

Vocabulary

un appel aux émotions an appeal to the emotions

bouillant boiling

émotif emotive

une épée sword

étincelant sparkling

l'exagération (f) exaggeration

une expression rhétorique rhetorical expression

une lame blade

la métaphore metaphor

le nom abstrait abstract noun

le symbole symbol

le vocabulaire sophistiqué sophisticated vocabulary

Trial vocabulary:

le banc d'accusé the dock

la barre witness box

l'instruction (f) investigation (in preparation for a trial)

l'interrogatoire (m) questioning

la plaidoirie summing up (by the lawyers at the end of the trial)

le pourvoi appeal (against a verdict)

le prétoire audience seating in the courtroom

la suspension recess

la tribune rostrum (judge's seating in the courtroom)

Useful phrases

sa façon de parler est simple / complexe / brutale he has a simple / complex / violent way of speaking

Examinons le style du narrateur… Let us examine the narrator's style…

Le balcon sert à symboliser… The balcony serves to symbolise…

…est hautement symbolique… …is highly symbolic…

Camus choisit le langage métaphorique / figuratif Camus chooses to use metaphorical language

L'utilisation d'expressions rhétoriques, comme par exemple… The use of rhetorical expressions, such as…

son caractère / son humeur s'exprime à travers son choix de mots his personality / mood is expressed in his choice of words

Une courte citation peut démontrer que… A short quotation can show that…

l'utilisation du passé composé par le narrateur dans son récit the narrator's use of the perfect tense in his narrative

de courtes phrases dépourvues de structures grammaticales complexes short sentences without complex grammatical structures

Sense impressions

For most of the novel, Meursault doesn't say much about what he thinks or feels emotionally, but he does tell us what he sees, hears, smells and touches, and notes pleasant and unpleasant sensations. Often these sense impressions are the only thing that is happening in the story. Meursault is not actually doing anything, just passively taking in the world around him. In the second chapter of the novel, for instance, the 'action' largely consists of Meursault sitting alone on his balcony with descriptions in the text of the sights and sounds of the street below as afternoon fades to evening.

Activité 1

Relisez l'épisode du balcon *(Part I, Chapter 2)*. Quelles sont les principales impressions visuelles et auditives notées par Meursault? Trouvez-vous des références à ses autres sens pendant l'épisode?

Physical sensations have a strong effect on Meursault, and he attaches importance to them. He likes washing his hands in the office bathroom at lunchtime, but not at the end of the day, because by that time the roller-towel feels damp. He raises this as an issue with his boss. The boss dismisses it as **'un détail sans importance'** *(Part I, Chapter 3)*, but it is clearly not an unimportant detail to Meursault.

Heat and the sun

L'Étranger's reputation as a **philosophical novel** about human life in general can sometimes make us forget that it's a novel set in a very real and particular place: Algeria. Many of the sense impressions in the book are particularly related to the sun in Algeria. Most of these impressions are positive, and create a strong contrast to Meursault's unhappy memories of Paris, which he remembers as the dark, dirty abode of sun-deprived northerners.

philosophical novel *le roman philosophique* a novel that draws on or illustrates ideas about the nature of knowledge, reality and existence (philosophy). Other famous French philosophical novels include *Candide* by Voltaire and *La Nausée* by Jean-Paul Sartre

---

« C'est sale. Il y a des pigeons et des cours noires. Les gens ont la peau blanche. »
(Part I, Chapter 5)

J'avais tout le ciel dans les yeux et il était bleu et doré. Sous ma nuque, je sentais le ventre de Marie battre doucement. Nous sommes restés longtemps sur la bouée, à moitié endormis.
(Part I, Chapter 2)

On two occasions, the day after the funeral and the day of the shooting, we see Meursault sunbathing at the beach. Meursault enjoys the look and feel of Marie's body at the beach. As they sunbathe together he is lulled by **'les deux chaleurs de son corps et du soleil'** *(Part I, Chapter 6)*. By linking her warm body to the warmth of the sun, Meursault emphasises the physical aspect of their relationship. For Meursault, the happiness you can get from being with another human being is really not that different from the happiness you get from the feeling of warm sand on your skin. The nature of Meursault and Marie's relationship is discussed in more depth in the *Characters* section (pages 39–40).

 Activité 2

Traduisez cet extrait.

 Au large, nous avons fait la planche et sur mon visage tourné vers le ciel le soleil écartait les derniers voiles d'eau qui me coulaient dans la bouche. Nous avons vu que Masson regagnait la plage pour s'étendre au soleil. De loin, il paraissait énorme. Marie a voulu que nous nagions ensemble. Je me suis mis derrière elle pour la prendre par la taille et elle avançait à la force des bras pendant que je l'aidais en battant des pieds.

(Part I, Chapter 6)

As well as morning sunshine at the beach, cool summer evenings are also positively remarked on by Meursault, and remembered longingly from the prison *(Part II, Chapter 4)*. But the fierce sun of an Algerian summer at midday is quite a different matter.

> **Key quotations**
>
> **Je me suis réveillé avec des étoiles sur le visage. Des bruits de campagne montaient jusqu'à moi. Des odeurs de nuit, de terre et de sel rafraîchissaient mes tempes. La merveilleuse paix de cet été endormi entrait en moi comme une marée.** *(Part II, Chapter 5)*
>
> **Le soleil tombait presque d'aplomb sur le sable et son éclat sur la mer était insoutenable. Il n'y avait plus personne sur la plage. […] On respirait à peine dans la chaleur de pierre qui montait du sol.** *(Part I, Chapter 6)*

Meursault experiences the full force of the midday sun at two points in the story: on the walk to his mother's burial and during the brawl and shooting on the beach with the Arabs. Both times, the novel emphasises how the light and heat completely overwhelm all of Meursault's senses. He excuses his inappropriate behaviour at his mother's funeral by explaining to his lawyer, 'j'avais une nature telle que mes besoins physiques dérangeaient souvent mes sentiments' *(Part II, Chapter 1)* and later in the courtroom, he claims that the shooting itself happened 'à cause du soleil' *(Part I, Chapter 4).* As we will see later in the section on *Freedom* (page 73), the account of the killing suggests this may be literally true.

Activité 3

Cherchez cinq références à la chaleur ou à la lumière du soleil dans le roman. Quelles images Meursault utilise-t-il pour évoquer le soleil? Comment décrit-il les effets de la chaleur et de la lumière sur son corps et sur son cerveau? Dans les références que vous avez trouvées, le soleil est-il représenté de manière positive ou négative?

Writing about the natural world

Make sure you revise the vocabulary related to the natural world on page 79 to prepare you for your exam. Being able to use accurate and precise vocabulary in your analysis will help you make your points more successfully.

Religion and atheism

The theme of belief in God, and the lack of it, emerges slowly in *L'Étranger*. There is a brief reference in the opening pages, when Meursault is told that his mother is to have a religious burial, as her fellow residents claim she wished. Meursault comments: 'Maman, sans être athée, n'avait jamais pensé de son vivant à la religion' *(Part I, Chapter 1).*

This shows that Meursault has had a non-religious upbringing, which in his case has led to unambiguous **atheism**. It also, reminds us of the different attitude to religion in France and its colonies compared to most other Western countries at the time. In France, religious burials are not the only option, or even the expected option, for a funeral, unlike the UK in this period. The French principle of **state secularism** limits the role of religion in public life, and in theory makes the kind of non-religious life Meursault chooses to lead socially acceptable and unproblematic. This secularism extends to the justice system in which Meursault becomes involved in the second half of the novel. Nobody in French courtrooms swears on the Bible, for instance, as people still do in the UK and the US. Both the *juge d'instruction* and the chaplain, then, are actually behaving inappropriately when they confront Meursault about religion. The *juge d'instruction* is an agent of the state and has no business discussing religion with suspects. The prison chaplain imposes himself and his beliefs on Meursault, despite Meursault's repeated insistence that he does not want to talk to him.

Activité 4

Qui sont les personnages dans la deuxième partie du roman qui se déclarent croyants? Qu'apprenons-nous sur leur foi? Quelle est leur attitude envers Meursault?

In the scene with the *juge d'instruction (Part II, Chapter 1)*, Meursault is asked to **repent** for his crime in order to be forgiven. The *juge d'instruction* blends together legal and religious ideas about guilt, confession and punishment, and puts himself in the role of a priest with a sinner rather than a magistrate with a suspect. When Meursault rejects this approach by saying he does not believe in God, the response is furious.

> **atheism** *l'athéisme (m)* not believing that a god or gods exist
>
> **state secularism** *la laïcité* the policy that religion should not be involved in the government or public life of a country
>
> **repent** *repentir* to feel or express sincere regret for wrongdoing. The term has strong religious connotations, implying remorse for behaviour that is considered sinful

---

Key quotation

Mais il m'a coupé et m'a exhorté une dernière fois, dressé de toute sa hauteur, en me demandant si je croyais en Dieu. J'ai répondu que non. Il s'est assis avec indignation. Il m'a dit que c'était impossible, que tous les hommes croyaient en Dieu, même ceux qui se détournaient de son visage.
(Part II, Chapter 1)

Note that the way the *juge d'instruction* recasts Meursault's response turns it from a straightforward true-or-false question into one of morality. For Meursault it is a simple question of fact: does God exist, yes or no? He has decided the answer is 'no', based, as the end of the story reveals, on his experience of what life is all about. For the *juge d'instruction*, it is inconceivable that Meursault might genuinely think that there is no God. He must have made a deliberate decision to turn away from God, the *juge d'instruction* thinks, and towards evil, in the knowledge that he is abandoning truth and goodness.

It is in the second of these religious encounters that Meursault is finally able to express his own views. The chaplain suggests that Meursault is too attached to his earthly life, and not focused enough on the possibility of salvation and eternal life in heaven. Meursault freely admits to wishing that there was such a thing as an afterlife, but wishing, he implies, doesn't make it any more likely to be true. The chaplain asks if he lives with no hope of salvation, in the belief that death is the absolute end, and he replies that he does.

It is when the chaplain asks why Meursault will not call him 'father', and then says that he will pray for him, that something 'bursts' inside Meursault (**'il y a quelque chose qui a crevé en moi'** *Part II, Chapter 5*) and he begins to shout his own world view.

He starts by talking about the difference between faith, which is what the chaplain has, and real certainty, which is what he has.

Key quotation

Il avait l'air si certain, n'est-ce pas? Pourtant, aucune de ses certitudes ne valait un cheveu de femme. Il n'était même pas sûr d'être en vie puisqu'il vivait comme un mort. Moi, j'avais l'air d'avoir les mains vides. Mais j'étais sûr de moi, sûr de tout, plus sûr que lui, sûr de ma vie et de cette mort qui allait venir.
(Part II, Chapter 5)

Meursault suggests that the chaplain **'vivait comme un mort'** *(Part II, Chapter 5)*. This is probably in part a criticism of the Catholic priest's vow of celibacy. For Meursault, sex is an important part of life, and by abstaining from sex, he believes the chaplain is failing to live life to the full. But beyond that, there's a wider and more important accusation. Meursault is claiming that religion encourages people to value their faith in an afterlife over their experience of life in this world. His own view of existence is that this life is all he has and that death, which is certainly awaiting him, will snuff out his consciousness entirely and forever.

He argues that this keeps him focused on the life that he has, and encourages him to experience it as fully as possible. All that he knows for sure is that he's alive now and that he will die in the future. The hope and faith that the chaplain urges him to embrace is a distraction from this, especially now that he has so little time left to be alive.

The shooting, from Jacques Ferrandez's graphic novel

The value of life

The later parts of his speech to the chaplain take a darker turn. He argues that the fact we're all going to die means that we're all equal in the face of this shared fate. However, he also seems to argue that it means that what happens in life before we die doesn't matter. A few pages earlier he told us 'Mais tout le monde sait que la vie ne vaut pas la peine d'être vécue' (Part II, Chapter 5). Now he seems to be saying that, since everyone is going to die anyway, nothing in life matters; that Salamano's dog was worth as much as his wife, and that other people's deaths don't matter.

This is a troubling thing for a convicted killer to say, and we'll return to it shortly in the *Morality* section (page 74). Before we look at the morality of taking another person's life, though, let us look more closely at the implications of Meursault's speech for his own life. Is Camus really using Meursault to tell us that life is pointless and not worth living?

That's unlikely for several reasons. First, as we saw in the *Context* section (page 26), Camus was writing a philosophical essay, *Le Mythe de Sisyphe*, at the same time as *L'Étranger*, and that essay was specifically about the question of whether life is worth living, as it lays out in its opening lines:

> **Key quotation**
>
> Il n'y a qu'un problème philosophique vraiment sérieux: c'est le suicide. Juger que la vie vaut ou ne vaut pas la peine d'être vécue, c'est répondre à la question fondamentale de la philosophie.
> (*Le Mythe de Sisyphe*)

Le Mythe de Sisyphe reaches a very clear answer to the question: yes, life is worth living. Yes, it's worth living even in a godless, meaningless universe in which we know that death is coming for us some day. What's more, Camus argues, is that life is especially worth living with our eyes open, facing up to our 'absurd' situation, rather than deluding ourselves with a belief in divine purpose or salvation to make ourselves feel better.

Do we see a similar attitude in Meursault? His speech to the chaplain seems a good deal more negative, but consider its context. Meursault is deprived of freedom, under threat of imminent execution, and his patience has been tested to the limit by the chaplain's condescension. Anger and despair are understandable reactions in this situation. A page or so later, the novel ends on an altogether calmer and more positive note.

As in the balcony scene near the start of the novel, the cool of a summer evening brings a **'merveilleuse paix'** *(Part II, Chapter 5)* to Meursault. He repeats the description of summer evenings as **'une trêve mélancolique'** which he also used in the first chapter of the first half, with reference to the old people's home. This leads him to understand why his mother took a boyfriend at the very end of her life, saying she must have felt **'libérée et prête à tout revivre'** *(Part II, Chapter 5)*. With his own death now imminent, Meursault says that he too feels ready to live his life all over again. The end of the novel confirms what we saw in the first half: the life Meursault was leading as a free man may have been solitary and out-of-step with society, but it was a contented life filled with small pleasures, and it was not worthless.

Activité 5

Quelles sont les différences entre la vision du monde exprimée par Meursault dans **sa diatribe** contre l'aumônier et les sentiments qu'il décrit dans les dernières pages du roman, lorsqu'il est de nouveau seul dans sa cellule? Quelles caractéristiques dans la liste suivante les distinguent?

- optimisme / pessimisme
- calme / fureur
- espoir / désespoir
- passion / tranquillité
- haine / bonheur

À votre avis, y a-t-il une contradiction? Est-ce que ce que Meursault dit à l'aumônier est en désaccord avec ce qu'il pense à la fin du roman?

diatribe / tirade *la diatribe / la tirade* a long, angry speech, usually denouncing or condemning something

Religious parallels

One final point about religious themes in the novel comes from its very last line:

> **Key quotation**
>
> Pour que tout soit consommé, pour que je me sente moins seul, il me restait à souhaiter qu'il y ait beaucoup de spectateurs le jour de mon exécution et qu'ils m'accueillent avec des cris de haine.
> *(Part II, Chapter 5)*

Both the scene he conjures up and the idea that a scene like this would somehow 'consummate' or fulfil his story or his life, is reminiscent of the Christian New Testament, in which Jesus's crucifixion is a necessary part of God's plan to redeem humanity, and in which Jesus is mocked and rejected by crowds of people in the course of his trial and execution. The similarity is no coincidence. When Camus added a preface to the novel for a later edition aimed at American university students, he wrote about Meursault as a Christ-like figure.

> **Key quotation**
>
> J'avais essayé de figurer dans mon personnage le seul christ que nous méritions.
> *(Préface à l'édition universitaire américaine)*

(Note that 'méritions' is in the subjunctive mood in the above quotation, i.e. 'that we might deserve'.)

Camus says that he isn't trying to be **blasphemous** in making this claim, and relates it to the fact that Meursault 'accepte de mourir pour la vérité' *(Préface à l'édition universitaire américaine)*, albeit in a different sense, and for a different truth, from the way Jesus might be said to have done so. Meursault is given several opportunities to lie his way out of trouble during the court case, by claiming that he feels remorse about the shooting, for instance, or saying that he was bottling up his grief during the funeral. He chooses to die rather than save his skin through dishonesty and in that, Camus suggests, Meursault is setting us an example.

blasphemous *blasphématoire* insulting, or showing contempt or lack of reverence for God

Race and colonialism

L'Étranger was written and is set in a colonial society. Its characters are made up of both French-Algerian colonists and Algerian Arabs, and its plot centres on a conflict between members of these two communities that culminates in a white colonist shooting an Arab man dead. Reading it today, we can't avoid being constantly aware of the issues of race and colonisation in the situation that the novel describes. But whether race and colonialism are themes in *L'Étranger* is an issue for debate.

Although they are important to the novel's plot, the Arab characters receive little attention in the story:

- We are not told the name of Raymond's mistress: Meursault tells us only, 'Quand il m'a dit le nom de la femme, j'ai vu que c'était une Mauresque' *(Part I, Chapter 3)*. ('Mauresque' is a dated term used by French colonists to refer to Arab people, related to the English 'Moorish'.)
- We see the mistress briefly in Chapter 4 when the policeman is called to stop Raymond's assault on her, but are given no description of her, and not even told if she has visible injuries.
- Her brother is also unnamed, although his name must surely have been repeatedly mentioned during the trial.
- Camus does not give him a single line of dialogue in any of his four appearances in the novel, even though we know from Raymond that he speaks French.
- Meursault makes no reference to the brother's legitimate grievance against Raymond.
- It's often unclear which of the two Arab men who follow Raymond to the beach is actually the brother of the abused woman.

When we looked at the Arab man as a character on page 45, it was suggested that he might be more of a plot device; a means to get Meursault on trial for his lifestyle rather than a proper character in his own right. If that's true, what are we to think about a colonial novel that uses its Arab characters as plot devices for its white characters' drama? Does that make it a racist book?

The novel does offer a positive portrait of the Arabs in the holding cell with Meursault after his arrest. Meursault seems as much a part of a community with them as he has ever been with anyone.

It is fair to say, though, that Meursault is a man of his time: the European settlers led a largely parallel existence to the Arab community, with only limited interest in and empathy for their neighbours. Camus's work as a journalist campaigning for social justice towards Arab communities may have given him greater knowledge and a more enlightened attitude than many other French-Algerians, but Meursault and the other white characters in the novel are typical in their detachment and disregard for Arabs and Arab culture.

Activité 6

Imaginez quatre lecteurs de *L'Étranger*: un lecteur français et un lecteur algérien d'aujourd'hui, et un lecteur européen et un lecteur arabe des années 40. À votre avis, quelles seraient leurs réactions aux personnages et aux événements du roman? Que penseraient-ils de Meursault?

Meursault: contre-enquête

If you're interested in this aspect of the story, then you might be interested to read *Meursault: contre-enquête* by the Algerian novelist Kamel Daoud. It has the clever premise that *L'Étranger* was actually not a novel but an autobiography by Meursault himself, and that the Arab man had a younger brother Haroun (Daoud's narrator), who is anxious to right the injustice of his brother's death. Haroun seems even more angry with Meursault for marginalising his brother in the story, to the extent of not bothering to tell the reader his name.

As the story continues however, Haroun finds his own life comes to resemble Meursault's in unexpected ways. Finally, as he finds his own freedom to live his life as he wishes curtailed in post-independence Algeria, he finds himself quoting Meursault's own words from his final tirade, with an imam in the place of the prison chaplain.

Outsider status

Meursault is an outsider in two main ways. One is that he doesn't play by the rules of society. Camus himself discusses this in the preface to the American edition: 'le héros du livre est condamné parce qu'il ne joue pas le jeu. En ce sens, il est étranger à la société où il vit, il erre, en marge, dans les faubourgs de la vie privée, solitaire, sensuelle' *(Préface à l'édition universitaire américaine)*.

Not only does he smoke cigarettes, drink coffee and fail to cry at his mother's funeral, but he is also out of step in smaller ways. He is not ambitious at work. He does not go to church, nor even pretend to have religious feelings. He thinks choosing whether to get married is unimportant. Finally, he will not put any kind of spin on the truth, not to spare other people's feelings, nor to save his own life.

The second way he is an outsider is in his personal relationships. He is a loner, but not lonely. We infer that the way we see him spending his time at the start of the novel is typical for him: going to the beach alone, or making himself a meal for one, then sitting on his balcony. We saw in the *Language* section (page 56) how the balcony above the street might be seen as a symbol of his detachment.

Activité 7

Imaginez la journée parfaite selon Meursault. Que ferait-il? Justifiez votre réponse en faisant référence non seulement à ce qu'il fait pendant la première partie du roman, mais aussi à ce qui lui manque et à ce qu'il regrette lorsqu'il est en prison.

He does not seem to have any real friends. Raymond, a neighbour, and Céleste, the owner of the restaurant where Meursault often eats, do call themselves Meursault's friends. However, Raymond only does so after he's persuaded Meursault to write his revenge-plot letter for him, and Meursault himself does not care whether he is Raymond's friend.

> **Key quotation**
>
> « Maintenant, tu es un vrai copain » [...]. Il a répété sa phrase et j'ai dit: « Oui. » Cela m'était égal d'être son copain et il avait vraiment l'air d'en avoir envie.
> *(Part I, Chapter 3)*

Céleste's declaration of friendship is similarly unconvincing: the prosecutor at the trial asks him if Meursault was a customer, to which he defensively replies « Oui, mais c'était aussi un ami » *(Part II, Chapter 3)*.

Meursault's relationship with Marie only bolsters his outsider status. He appreciates her body and enjoys their sexual relationship, as well as finding her cheerful nature attractive, but there is little to their relationship beyond this. It doesn't occur to him to take an interest in what she does when she's not with him. He regards the decision to get married as unimportant, and suggests that he considers Marie interchangeable with other women.

Meursault displays a lack of sensitivity or curiosity towards other people's feelings; he is uncommunicative, saying little, and sometimes being hurtfully blunt when he does speak. He lacks social skills, avoids company, and doesn't follow the norms of social behaviour. All of these attributes have led some critics to see parallels between his personality and character traits associated with autism.

Activité 8

1. Lisez cette liste de traits de personnalité associés aux troubles du spectre autistique:

   - des difficultés dans le domaine des relations et des interactions sociales: se faire des amis, comprendre les règles tacites de conduite sociale et les conventions sociales, attribuer à autrui des pensées ou se représenter un état émotionnel
   - une difficulté à reconnaître les émotions et à les gérer
   - des particularités dans la communication verbale et non verbale: ton de la voix, façon rigide de s'exprimer, difficulté à comprendre les métaphores, le sens figuré, l'ironie, mauvais contact visuel, difficulté dans la conversation et la réciprocité émotionnelle
   - dans le domaine de la compréhension: le détail prime sur le global, difficulté d'accès au sens, une compréhension essentiellement par des moyens visuels ou tactiles et non abstraits
   - des intérêts restreints (en nombre ou très forts en intensité, répétition de cet intérêt)
   - de la maladresse motrice
   - un besoin de routine et une difficulté d'adaptation aux changements et aux imprévus, une tendance aux comportements répétés et stéréotypés
   - des perceptions sensorielles souvent exacerbées, par exemple hypersensibilité au bruit, à la lumière, aux odeurs, intolérance à certaines textures.

   (Source: Groupe Asperger, Switzerland)

2. Combien de ces traits de caractère s'accordent avec la personnalité de Meursault? Cherchez des exemples dans le texte pour valider votre réponse. Quels traits ne s'accordent pas avec Meursault?

3. Pensez-vous que Meursault puisse être atteint d'un trouble neurologique, ce qui expliquerait son statut d'étranger dans sa communauté? Ou croyez-vous que c'est tout simplement un homme qui a librement choisi sa vie d'étranger?

The outsider and the Absurd

Meursault's outsider status helps us understand the philosophical remarks at the very end of the novel:

> **Key quotation**
>
> [J]e m'ouvrais pour la première fois à la tendre indifférence du monde. De l'éprouver si pareil à moi, si fraternel enfin, j'ai senti que j'avais été heureux, et que je l'étais encore.
> *(Part II, Chapter 5)*

These lines, which echo the final sentence of *Le Mythe de Sisyphe*, 'Il faut imaginer Sisyphe heureux', end the novel on a positive note about the precious value of life, but at the same time seem very **paradoxical**.

> **paradox** *le paradoxe* a statement that seems self-contradictory or absurd, but in fact is intended to express a truth. For example: 'Sometimes, you have to be cruel to be kind'

How can indifference be 'tender'? And if the world is indifferent towards Meursault, how can it also be 'fraternal'? 'Indifferent' suggests not caring at all about someone, while 'fraternal' suggests caring as if for a brother. These two attitudes would seem to be more or less opposite to each other. The answer is perhaps that Meursault thinks the world is fraternal because it is more like him than it is like other people.

As we saw in the *Context* section 'Existentialism and the Absurd' on page 31, Meursault is detached and indifferent, happy to get on with his own thing and let other people get on with theirs. He doesn't ask anything of anyone, and he does not want to be responsible for anyone. Other people may follow rules, make commitments, have purpose in their lives, and live with close social and emotional ties to others, but not Meursault.

And here at the end of the story, he is rejecting the idea that we're living in a divinely created universe, filled with God's love for us, made especially for us, and with a deep connection to and purpose for each of us. The universe doesn't care about us, Meursault thinks. It has no need of us, no plans for us, and no love for us. It does not want us to worship it. It doesn't want us to do anything. We are free to live our lives however we want, and the world will let us do so.

The world, then, is like Meursault, not like the people who condemn him.

Freedom

L'Étranger is a novel of freedom and confinement, and the two parts of the story make a strict division between them. In the first half, Meursault is free of commitments and lives life as he pleases. When he's not at work, his time is his own, to spend enjoying himself at the beach, the cinema or quietly on his balcony. He also likes to be spontaneous.

> **Key quotation**
>
> Pendant que je me rasais, je me suis demandé ce que j'allais faire et j'ai décidé d'aller me baigner.
> *(Part I, Chapter 2)*

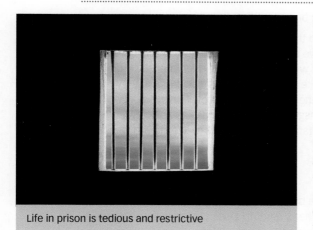

Life in prison is tedious and restrictive

Rather than make plans, join clubs, or keep to a schedule, Meursault prefers to keep his time free so that he can do whatever he happens to be in the mood for at any one time. This is one reason why he is not keen on a move to Paris for a role with more money and responsibility. It may also be why he is not enthusiastic about getting engaged to Marie, although he agrees to do so to make her happy.

In the second half of the novel, the only locations are interrogation rooms, the courtroom, and the prison. The change from the open spaces, the light and air of the first half is drastic. Camus emphasises it by skipping over the cooler months of Meursault's year to focus on the hot, airless summer heat, where the atmosphere in the courtroom feels unbearably oppressive. Elsewhere, a lot of attention is paid to the tedium and restriction of life in a prison cell, which Meursault explicitly compares to his former liberty:

> **Key quotation**
>
> Au début de ma détention, pourtant, ce qui a été le plus dur, c'est que j'avais des pensées d'homme libre. Par exemple, l'envie me prenait d'être sur une plage et de descendre vers la mer. À imaginer le bruit des premières vagues sous la plante de mes pieds, l'entrée du corps dans l'eau et la délivrance que j'y trouvais, je sentais tout d'un coup combien les murs de ma prison étaient rapprochés.
> *(Part II, Chapter 2)*

Activité 9

Cherchez des références à la baignade dans le roman. Est-ce qu'elles sont liées au concept de liberté, comme dans la citation à la page 73? Pensez-vous que la baignade soit un symbole de liberté dans le roman? Si oui, pourquoi Camus aurait-il choisi cette métaphore?

As well as Meursault being literally a free man and a prisoner, the theme of freedom and restriction takes on a wider resonance in the story. In fact, the whole court case, once it has sidelined the killing itself, becomes a trial about whether people should be free to do as they want, even if what they want to do is different from other people and seen as inappropriate. Meursault's failure to cry at his mother's funeral didn't hurt anyone else, but, according to the prosecutor's point of view, it broke a rule about how people are expected to behave. He <u>ought</u> to have cried.

Similarly, his swimming and cinema trip the following day are things that, according to the prosecution, he ought not to have done. The judge and jury agree. Camus suggests that society's expectations of what we ought and ought not to be doing restrict our freedom. When someone like Meursault comes along who simply does what he likes, not caring about other people's disapproval, then society is outraged and punishes him for the transgression. At the end of the story, Meursault appreciates the freedom he had, and stands up for his right to live life the way he wanted to live it.

Morality

Is Meursault a bad person? If so, is he a bad person because he killed someone, or because of how he behaved at his mother's funeral? Does Camus want us to make up our own minds about the answer, or is he trying to nudge us towards a 'correct' view of Meursault that the novel endorses?

The novel certainly has no shortage of people telling us that Meursault is a bad person. The *juge d'instruction* and the prosecutor in particular present him as a heartless monster, who neither knows nor cares about the difference between right and wrong.

Key quotation

« [L]e vide du cœur tel qu'on le découvre chez cet homme devient un gouffre où la société peut succomber. »
(Part II, Chapter 4)

Camus doesn't seem to be encouraging us to adopt their point of view, however. They are aggressive, moralistic, unfair and sometimes ridiculous, waving a crucifix in Meursault's face, twisting the facts to present him in the worst possible light, or making an absurdly big deal about something as small as accepting a cup of coffee.

But there are other reasons too to see Meursault negatively. More trustworthy and sympathetic characters can also see him this way, as shown by Marie's **'petit recul'** *(Part I, Chapter 2)* on discovering that the man who has been swimming and flirting with her is supposedly in mourning. There are Meursault's own actions too. You may well agree that some of the things he does are thoughtless, inappropriate, or even immoral. He participates in Raymond's 'revenge' scheme, for instance, in full knowledge of the humiliation prepared for Raymond's mistress. And, of course, he not only shoots the Arab man on the beach, perhaps accidentally, but also shoots four further bullets into the body, in what can hardly be a slip of the finger.

Activité 10

Analyse du caractère de Meursault

1. Lisez ces dix opinions sur le caractère de Meursault, exprimées par les autres personnages du roman et par Meursault lui-même.

Opinion	Personnage
a) Je savais bien que tu connaissais la vie *(Part I, Chapter 3)*.	
b) Elle a murmuré que j'étais bizarre *(Part I, Chapter 5)*.	
c) On me dépeignait comme étant d'un caractère taciturne et renfermé *(Part II, Chapter 1)*.	
d) J'avais fait preuve d'insensibilité *(Part II, Chapter 1)*.	
e) J'avais un peu perdu l'habitude de m'interroger *(Part II, Chapter 1)*.	
f) Mes besoins physiques dérangeaient souvent mes sentiments *(Part II, Chapter 1)*.	
g) J'étais comme tout le monde, absolument comme tout le monde *(Part II, Chapter 1)*.	
h) On lui a demandé […] ce qu'il pensait de moi et il a répondu que j'étais un homme *(Part II, Chapter 3)*.	
i) Un cœur de criminel *(Part II, Chapter 3)*.	
j) Il disait qu'à la vérité, je n'en avais point, d'âme, et que rien d'humain, et pas un des principes moraux qui gardent le cœur des hommes ne m'était accessible *(Part II, Chapter 4)*.	

2. Trouvez le personnage qui correspond à chacune des dix opinions.

3. Sélectionnez une opinion de la liste. Expliquez ce que le personnage a voulu dire sur le caractère de Meursault. Êtes-vous d'accord avec cette opinion de Meursault?

Lastly, there is what Meursault says himself, which can sometimes be disturbing.

> **Key quotations**
>
> [P]lutôt que du regret véritable, j'éprouvais un certain ennui.
> *(Part II, Chapter 1)*
>
> Que m'importaient la mort des autres, l'amour d'une mère [...] puisqu'un seul destin devait m'élire moi-même et avec moi des milliards de privilégiés qui, comme [l'aumônier], se disaient mes frères.
> *(Part II, Chapter 5)*

On more than one occasion, he says that he feels no remorse for the killing. We might argue that, if it was a simple accident, there is nothing to feel guilty about. On the other hand, the attitude seems dismissive, and at no point does Meursault give any thought to the life his victim might have lived or the suffering of his sister and other family left behind. More worryingly, in his tirade to the chaplain, Meursault says that, since we are all going to die at some point anyway, then other people's deaths don't matter to him. It may be said in the heat of the moment, when Meursault is overcome with anger and despair, but it could be interpreted that he doesn't see killing people as necessarily wrong. His final remarks on the value of life and the happiness of his own experience may counter-balance such **nihilism**, but they do not entirely dispel it.

Activité 11

Traduisez cet extrait.

Je crois que j'ai dormi parce que je me suis réveillé avec des étoiles sur le visage. Des bruits de campagne montaient jusqu'à moi. Des odeurs de nuit, de terre et de sel rafraîchissaient mes tempes. La merveilleuse paix de cet été endormi entrait en moi comme une marée. À ce moment, et à la limite de la nuit, des sirènes ont hurlé. Elles annonçaient des départs pour un monde qui maintenant m'était à jamais indifférent. Pour la première fois depuis bien longtemps, j'ai pensé à maman.

(Part II, Chapter 5)

nihilism *le nihilisme* a rejection of all morality, and a belief that life is worthless

What, on the other hand, might make us see Meursault as a good man? Most of the behaviour he is actually condemned for harmed nobody. He is sentenced to death for being different. In his everyday life he works hard ('**J'ai bien travaillé toute la semaine'** *Part I, Chapter 4*), causes no trouble, and gets on with other people. He is happy to help, and willing to do whatever will please other people, something which may be a good thing where Marie is concerned, but less so with Raymond. Most importantly, he is an honest person. He can be relied upon to tell the truth, no matter what the consequences. During the court case, dishonesty is repeatedly encouraged. His lawyer wishes to misrepresent his feelings at the funeral. He is condemned in the courtroom for not faking a sadness he did not feel. At any moment, it is implied, he could save his own skin by pretending to feel grief about his mother and remorse about the Arab man. Yet he will not do either, even if this honesty will lead to his execution.

This aspect of the story is one that Camus himself highlighted when discussing the meaning of the novel:

Key quotation

J'ai résumé *L'Étranger*, il y a longtemps, par une phrase dont je reconnais qu'elle est très paradoxale: « Dans notre société tout homme qui ne pleure pas à l'enterrement de sa mère risque d'être condamné à mort. » […] Il refuse de mentir. On ne se tromperait donc pas beaucoup en lisant dans *L'Étranger* l'histoire d'un homme qui, sans aucune attitude héroïque, accepte de mourir pour la vérité.
(Préface à l'édition universitaire américaine)

So, for Camus, it seems Meursault is a good man in this important respect at least.

Activité 12

Sartre, l'ami de Camus, a dit à propos du théâtre: « Une bonne pièce de théâtre doit poser des problèmes et non les résoudre. » À votre avis, le roman de Camus adopte-t-il la même approche?

Writing about themes

Often, an essay question will ask you specifically to analyse a particular theme of the novel. If this is the case, you need to show how the theme is expressed in the novel, as well as why it is important and what attitude the author or narrator takes towards it. To show how the theme is expressed, you should think about all the different elements of the novel which help to bring the theme to the fore.

- You can make reference to the <u>plot</u> of the novel to illustrate the theme of morality, for instance, by looking at how the events of the first half of the novel seem random when Meursault tells them, but are made to seem malicious and pre-meditated when retold in the courtroom.

- You could refer to the <u>structure</u> of the novel to discuss the theme of death, by pointing out how three different deaths mark the beginning, mid-point and end of the novel.

- You could discuss <u>character</u> to illustrate the theme of race / colonialism, by examining how the Arab characters are treated differently from the colonists.

- You could look at <u>narration</u> to discuss the theme of morality, by exploring how Meursault's simple, spontaneous storytelling reinforces the impression of his honesty.

- You could examine the <u>language</u> of the novel to analyse the theme of the natural world by exploring the metaphors associated with the sun in the shooting scene on the beach.

Even if a question does not ask directly about the themes of the novel, it will usually be relevant to include at least some reference to them. Any discussion of the *juge d'instruction* as a character should probably find room to mention the theme of religion and atheism, for instance.

Vocabulary

consommé fulfilled, consummated	**l'éclat (m)** brilliance
mériter to deserve	**éclatant** dazzling
la natte (sleeping) mat	**le frelon** hornet
The natural world:	**la marée** tide
d'aplomb (of sunshine) from directly overhead	**mouillé** damp
bourdonner to buzz (e.g. insects)	**l'ombre (f)** shade
la brûlure burning heat	**plonger** to dive (in)
la campagne countryside	**rafraîchir** to refresh, cool down
les chaleurs (fpl) hot weather	**le sable** sand
le cyprès cypress tree	**la vague** wave

Useful phrases

Pour aborder le thème de la nature...   To turn to the theme of the natural world…

une impression sensorielle / visuelle / auditive est créée   a sensory / visual / aural impression is created

l'importance du personnage de l'aumônier en ce qui concerne le thème de la religion   the importance of the character of the chaplain where the theme of religion is concerned

Ce thème est étroitement lié à...   This theme is closely connected to…

On ne peut pas parler du thème du colonialisme sans mentionner...   It is not possible to discuss the theme of colonialism without mentioning…

Ce thème est illustré par...   This theme is illustrated by…

Pour comprendre la représentation de la liberté dans le roman, il faut...   To understand the representation of freedom in the novel, it is necessary to…

l'attitude envers la religion exprimée dans le roman   the attitude towards religion expressed in the novel

J'insisterai tout particulièrement sur le thème de...   I will focus on the theme of…

Un épisode qui met ce thème en relief serait...   An episode which highlights this theme would be…

Camus souligne ce thème en écrivant...   Camus emphasises this theme by writing…

Outre cet élément, je voudrais aussi examiner le thème du / de l' / de la...   As well as this point, I would also like to examine the theme of…

Exam skills

Understanding the question

The exam questions will be written in French, which means there are two parts to understanding the question properly.

Firstly, you need to ask yourself whether you understand the vocabulary, grammar and structure of the French in the question, so that you can be confident you have correctly understood its basic meaning.

Secondly, you need to ask yourself what the question is getting at.

- What are you being asked to do? Analyse, explain, compare?
- What kind of conclusion do you need to be heading towards, and what do you need to consider along the way?
- What material from the novel are you being asked to examine?
- What contextual material do you need to draw on to answer the question properly, for example your knowledge of colonial Algeria, of Camus's own life, or of his philosophical ideas?
- What approach should you take to your material? A character study? A for-and-against argument?
- What perspective(s) should you be considering? Your own personal view, or a more objective reader's view? A view that might be held by someone within the world of the story, or from outside it? Should you speculate on how people might see things at the time of publication? Or how Camus saw things himself?

Vocabulary, grammar, and structure

If you have a choice of two questions, read both carefully. Make sure you have understood the French vocabulary correctly.

- Watch out for *faux amis*: 'attendre' does not mean 'to attend', 'blessé' is not 'blessed', 'une déception' is not 'a deception' (they're 'wait', 'injured' and 'a disappointment' respectively).

Look too at the grammar and structure of the sentence. Are you clear how the various parts of it fit together?

- Even if they're separated in the sentence, you can see which adjectives go with which nouns, and which subjects with which verbs, through agreements.
- Pay particular attention to the relative pronouns 'qui' and 'que'. 'L'homme **qui** tue Meursault' is the judicial executioner, the man who kills Meursault; 'l'homme **que** tue Meursault' is the Arab, the man whom Meursault kills. (The French phrases look so similar because relative clauses with 'que' can invert subject and verb, 'que Meursault tue' or 'que tue Meursault', with no change in meaning.)

Look especially at verb forms to be sure you have understood tense, mood and active or passive constructions. There's a lot of difference between 'il tue' (he kills), 'il est tué' (he is killed), 'il aurait tué' (he would have killed) and 'il n'aurait pas été tué' (he would not have been killed).

What if you're not sure? If you're unclear on the meaning of a particular word in the question, or confused by a grammatical construction, then there's a good chance you'll still be able to work out the meaning of the question. Use what you do recognise in the sentence to work out the most likely meaning of what you don't know. You can also use your knowledge of *L'Étranger* itself, e.g. the fact that it's Meursault who shoots the Arab and not the other way around, to unravel the structure of the question.

In the end, though, answering a question without properly understanding it is a big risk to take. No matter how clever, well-researched and well-written your answer is, if it isn't properly responding to the question that was asked, you will not get good marks. In a choice between two questions on *L'Étranger*, it will always be best to pick the one you're more confident of understanding precisely, even if it's not a topic you're keen to write about.

Question types

Next you need to decide what approach the question is asking you to take.

Many questions will begin by asking you to examine (**examinez**), explain (**expliquez**) analyse (**analysez**) or evaluate (**évaluez**). In all these cases you are being asked to explore a topic in detail, including evidence from the text and using contextual knowledge to demonstrate an understanding of the text.

In addition, **analysez** and **évaluez** are explicitly telling you that it's not enough to give information. You also need to interpret that information <u>from your own point of view</u>. That means that you're expected to construct an argument for your own interpretation of the novel's meaning, e.g. arguing that swimming in the novel is being used as a metaphor for freedom, or your own judgment on the characters, e.g. arguing that Meursault is guilty of manslaughter (*homicide involontaire*), but not murder.

Note that, while **examinez** and **expliquez** don't specifically say that you also need to give your own interpretation and construct an argument to support your views, in practice you should always do this in an exam essay. Always analyse and evaluate, even if the question doesn't use those exact words.

The Point, Evidence, Explanation (PEE) format can help you achieve this: when you make a point, support it with a quotation from the novel, then go on to explain and analyse its relevance to the argument you are making.

Other questions you may be asked include 'What is the role…?' (**Quel est le rôle…?**), 'How far / To what extent…?' (**Dans quelle mesure…?**), 'In what ways…?' (**De quelle manière… / De quelle façon…?**) and 'What is the impact…?' (**Quel est l'impact…?**). These questions draw attention to something else you should really be trying to do in answering any question, which is considering the answer from different points of view.

Points of view

If you are asked what role a character (or, indeed, anything else) plays in the story, then there are a number of angles you can approach this from.

- You can look at it from the character's own perspective. What are their aims? How do they set about achieving them?

- Then move outwards a step and explore the perspectives of other people in the story. How do they feel about the character? What kind of relationship do they have with them, and how do they interact?

- Then step back further and explore the character from the writer's perspective. Why do you think the writer included them in the book? What role do they have in moving the plot forward? What themes do they help to illustrate? How do they throw light on the main character through interactions, similarities and contrasts?

- Finally, there is the reader's perspective. Is the character sympathetic? Do we identify with them, root for them, pity them? Or perhaps fear or hate them?

Similarly, if you're asked about the ways in which the novel does something, even if French prefers the singular 'in what way...' (**de quelle manière / façon...**) to the English plural 'in what ways...', you're invited to look at several different ways.

As in the above example, you might look from the perspective of characters in the story, then the author, then the reader. Or, taking a different tack, you might examine the question with regard to the characters, then the plot of the novel, then the themes. For example, suppose you were answering the question: **Dans quelle mesure Meursault est-il coupable?**

- To explore it from the perspectives of characters, author, then reader, you might start by looking at the opinions of the lawyers and judges in the novel, and those of his friends. Then you might use the context of Camus's remarks comparing Meursault and Jesus as part of a discussion of the author's perspective. Lastly, you might bring in your own verdict on Meursault, and perhaps compare it with how you imagine a reader in the 1940s, or a non-European reader, would judge him.

- Looking at the same question from the perspective of characters, plot and themes would give you the same starting point, then perhaps lead you to look at how the plot of the first part of the novel is re-interpreted in the second to emphasise Meursault's guilt, and finally to explore the theme of morality, including Meursault's commitment to honesty and his acceptance to 'die for the truth'.

Often the best perspectives to use might simply be 'for' and 'against', as if arguing in a court case. When you're asked 'to what extent...' (**dans quelle mesure...**), you're expected to examine both 'for' and 'against' in detail, and to reach a nuanced conclusion that doesn't necessarily plump for one side or the other.

With the question **Dans quelle mesure Meursault est-il coupable?**, you are being asked to examine reasons why Meursault might be held responsible for the Arab man's death. As well as the obvious fact that he pulled the trigger, you might also look at his complicity in Raymond's abuse of the man's sister, and the fact that he continues to shoot bullets into the dead body.

Then you could look at the other side of the case, and find reasons that might absolve him of responsibility. Here you might explore the suggestion given at the trial that the killing was 'by chance', as well as Meursault's own claim that it was 'à cause du soleil'. You might also consider Meursault's character more generally and the circumstantial evidence, including that he took the gun to prevent Raymond from using it against the Arab man.

The conclusion you reach is unlikely to be that he is wholly innocent or entirely guilty, but you need to be able to explain where you place him in-between.

Activité 1

Choisissez une question dans la liste de questions AS ou A Level à la fin de ce chapitre (page 92). Quels sont les mots les plus importants dans la question? Quels éléments du roman – de son intrigue, ses personnages, ses thèmes, etc. – pourriez-vous utiliser dans votre réponse?

Tips for assessment

Two of the most common errors in exam essays are:

- spending time just telling the story to your reader instead of analysing it
- writing an essay that is about the correct topic, but doesn't respond properly to the specific question asked.

To avoid the first error, make sure you are always arguing and analysing, and that all the references to the novel are in support of a point you are making, not just there for their own sake.

The second error is a particular danger if you get a question in the exam on a similar topic to an essay you've already written while you were studying the novel. Don't be tempted to just re-use what you remember of that previous essay, as it's unlikely to be a good fit for the new question. Always make sure you read the question carefully and engage with it closely throughout your answer.

Planning your answer

It's definitely worth taking a few minutes of the exam to plan out your answer before you start to write it. When you are revising, you might be tempted to plan lots of different possible answers and then try to memorise the plans. In fact, this could harm your answer on the day. Trying to make an exam question 'fit' with a pre-planned answer will waste valuable time and distract you from the focus of the question you should be answering. You may miss key elements or spend too long on a minor point.

Examiners are looking for essays that really respond to the question that's been asked, precisely and in detail. That means you have to understand the central elements of the novel. Become familiar with the text, its characters, language, plot, themes, and context so that you can use the most relevant examples to support the points that you make in the most effective way.

You must also have thought carefully about all these things and developed your own opinions on them. You must have written practice essays, and practised writing plans, but don't try to learn the plans themselves. Instead, hone your skills at presenting your evidence and expressing your opinion on it in clear, elegant and accurate French. But what you also need on top of all this preparation is flexibility.

You need to be able to use your material flexibly to engage with the question that has been asked. Let's say you've been asked a question about Raymond Sintès:

> **Pensez-vous que Raymond soit le personnage le plus immoral du roman? Pourquoi / Pourquoi pas?**

To answer this question well, you need to plan an answer, jotting down what you know about Raymond that's relevant to the question, and leaving out what isn't. In this case, everything related to the question of whether he's a good or bad person is relevant; anything else is not. You can then use this material to answer the question.

Since the question asks you to consider the possibility that Raymond isn't the most immoral person in the book, you might combine this material with consideration of who else might be a candidate for the title: Meursault himself, perhaps, or maybe even the public prosecutor who twists the facts at the trial.

What you don't want to do is glance at the question, see that it mentions Raymond, and decide that means that you should put down everything you've carefully memorised about the character, whether or not it's relevant.

Even worse, it definitely doesn't mean that you should slap down a fully formed character-study that you've memorised word for word, perhaps with a line or two at the start and end to make it look like it's answering the question set. If your answer is too general, or doesn't properly fit the question, then you won't do well in the exam.

One of the most important – and most stressful – facts about essay-based exams is that, while revision and preparation is vitally important if you want to do well, you can't have everything prepared in advance. The material you're going to draw on needs to be ready in your mind, but the way that you draw on it can't be decided beforehand. It's true that the people who do best in the exam are usually those who have done the most careful and detailed preparation. It's also true, though, that success comes from a combination of preparation with intelligent use of your material on the day.

For the question on page 84, then, what material would you gather?

Linear plans

If you already have an idea of how the essay might be structured, you could use a linear plan to group your material under headings. It might look like the one below.

Raymond immoral

- Les voisins croient que c'est un maquereau.

- Il 'punit' sa maîtresse en lui crachant au visage et en l'agressant.

- Il demande à Meursault de tromper sa maîtresse et de mentir à la police.

- Il a l'intention de tirer sur l'Arabe à la plage. (Il en est dissuadé par Meursault.)

Raymond moral

- Son amitié pour Meursault est peut-être sincère. (?)

- Il reste loyal envers Meursault pendant le procès et tente d'affirmer son innocence.

Autres candidats pour le personnage le plus immoral
Meursault:

- Il tue l'Arabe à la plage et continue de tirer après l'avoir tué.

- Il aide Raymond quand celui-ci agresse sa maîtresse.

- Il n'éprouve ni remords pour la mort de l'Arabe ni tristesse après la mort de sa mère.

Mais...

- Il semble qu'il tue l'Arabe sans le vouloir.

- Son absence d'émotion et d'engagement social ne nuisent à personne.

- Il est très honnête.

Procureur:

- Il exagère et manipule les faits pour faire croire que Meursault a un « cœur de criminel ».

Mais...

- C'est un personnage plutôt mineur, qui ne fait que son travail.

Spider diagrams

You might want to make a spider diagram or a bullet point plan of the relevant points you can think of. This style of planning can be useful if you have a lot of ideas and want to jot them down in a visual way.

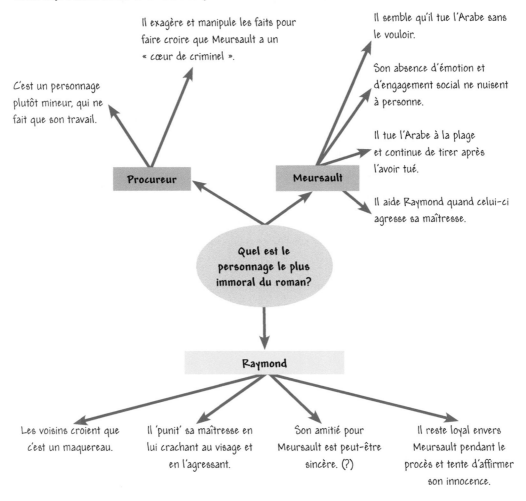

Il exagère et manipule les faits pour faire croire que Meursault a un « cœur de criminel ».

Il semble qu'il tue l'Arabe sans le vouloir.

C'est un personnage plutôt mineur, qui ne fait que son travail.

Son absence d'émotion et d'engagement social ne nuisent à personne.

Il tue l'Arabe à la plage et continue de tirer après l'avoir tué.

Procureur

Meursault

Il aide Raymond quand celui-ci agresse sa maîtresse.

Quel est le personnage le plus immoral du roman?

Raymond

Les voisins croient que c'est un maquereau.

Il 'punit' sa maîtresse en lui crachant au visage et en l'agressant.

Son amitié pour Meursault est peut-être sincère. (?)

Il reste loyal envers Meursault pendant le procès et tente d'affirmer son innocence.

While it might be tempting to write these notes in English for speed, it definitely makes more sense to do it in French. This way, you're already well on your way to having an essay expressed in good French: you simply need to expand on the points you already have. Also, writing your notes in French will make sure you don't get into the tricky position of making a particular point a key part of your argument, and then discovering that you don't know a vital piece of vocabulary so you can't express it in French, making your whole essay fall apart.

Lastly, it's worth thinking about other angles that might provide useful material for the essay. Consider how the question looks from the perspective of other characters, the writer and readers, for example.

Autres perspectives

- **Perspective judiciaire:** Raymond aussi est accusé d'un délit (l'agression de sa maîtresse). À la différence de Meursault, il n'est pas puni, parce qu'il sait « jouer le jeu ».
- **Perspective de l'écrivain:** Si Raymond est le personnage le plus immoral du roman, c'est peut-être pour servir de faire-valoir au héros du roman, Meursault.
- **Perspective du lecteur:** L'attitude des personnages européens (y compris Raymond et Meursault) envers les personnages arabes paraît plus choquante et plus immorale à un lecteur du 21ᵉ siècle qu'à un lecteur des années 40.

Points like these might be integrated into the main argument structure set out on page 85, or might feature in your introduction or conclusion. You might decide they're not sufficiently relevant or important compared with the other things you have to say, and leave them out. Remember, not everything in your plan has to be included in your final essay.

Tips for assessment

No matter how well you know the novel, and how well you can structure an argument, you won't do well in the exam unless you have the vocabulary to express what you want to say in the target language. Learning the French vocabulary you will need for the essay is probably the most important part of the revision process.

Consider making themed lists of vocabulary from the novel, relating to the trial, the natural world, the personalities of the characters, etc. Choose a dozen important words in each theme and work on a different word each day.

You will also need to work on learning the words and phrases you need to introduce your essay, argue points, present evidence and write a conclusion. Drawing up similar themed lists will help here.

Activité 2

Choisissez une question dans la liste de questions AS ou A Level à la page 92. Faites une liste ou un schéma en toile d'araignée de vos arguments en réponse. Quelles citations ou références au roman et à son contexte pouvez-vous utiliser à l'appui de vos arguments?

Writing your answer

Once you have your plan, you are ready to start writing your answer. Keep a rough idea in mind of how long you have to write, and how many words you are aiming for.

Divide your time evenly between the number of sections you want to write. If you are writing an essay with a for-and-against argument structure, then you ought to be allowing around half your time for the introduction and first part, and half your time for the second part and conclusion.

If your essay involves a wider approach, count the number of points you want to make from your plan, add the introduction and conclusion and divide your time roughly between each of them. It's very easy to see when an essay is unbalanced from spending too long on the early parts and then rushing the conclusion – or not even getting to a conclusion at all. It's also quite easy to make sure you don't get into this situation, as long as you're careful with your time.

While you can't have your whole argument prepared in advance, you can have a stock of French expressions stored up, which you can call on in order to present your material within a structured argument. The list at the end of this section (page 91) provides you with some examples.

Using Point, Evidence, Explanation

While you don't have to stick to it rigidly, the well-known formula for structuring paragraphs, Point, Evidence, Explanation (PEE), is just as useful for essays in French as in English. Look again at the question on Raymond's morality:

> **Pensez-vous que Raymond soit le personnage le plus immoral du roman? Pourquoi / Pourquoi pas?**

Here is a paragraph taken from a sample student's response to this question.

The student makes a clear statement in answer to the question.

They give evidence for their viewpoint by referring to the events of the story.

They strengthen their evidence with a short quotation from the text, which they link to their point.

Bien qu'il se présente comme un ami de Meursault, Raymond l'exploite pour se venger de sa maîtresse. Il est évident que Raymond invite Meursault chez lui et lui offre du vin uniquement pour le persuader de collaborer dans son projet d'humilier sa maîtresse. Lorsque Raymond dit à Meursault « Maintenant, tu es un vrai copain », Meursault remarque que ce tutoiement ne commence qu'après qu'il a écrit la lettre pour attirer la maîtresse de Raymond dans un piège. Cela suggère que Raymond n'est pas un vrai ami; il exploite Meursault par intérêt égoïste, sans se soucier de ce qui pourrait advenir à Meursault. Il est donc indirectement responsable de ce qui se passe par la suite.

The student finishes their paragraph with a clear explanation of how the quotation and the events of the story reveal Raymond to be an immoral character.

Using quotation effectively

Quotation can be a good way of providing evidence for the point you're making. It is more precise than paraphrase, and, if you have a quotation that relates closely to the argument you're making, there can be no stronger evidence for your case than the words of the author himself. When looking for quotations to memorise, always start with an idea of a point you might want to make in an essay, then go looking for the right quotation to back up that point. There's no point in learning a quotation unless you know exactly how you might use it. Even better, find a quotation you could use in several different essays, with relevance to more than one argument you might be making.

Don't memorise more of a quotation than you need to. If the evidence you want for your point is contained in three or four words, there's no point in memorising more. It will only take up more of your writing time, and you won't get extra credit for it. For instance, if you're describing Meursault's personality, there's no need to memorise all of the quotation used below (from Part II, Chapter 1).

> Lorsqu'il raconte son interrogatoire avec le juge d'instruction, Meursault nous informe qu' « il m'a d'abord dit qu'on me dépeignait comme étant d'un caractère taciturne et renfermé ».

You could simply say:

> Meursault a la réputation d'être « taciturne et renfermé ».

Achieving the best marks

To achieve high marks, your essay will need to demonstrate the following qualities:

- perceptive understanding of characters, themes, etc.
- responding to the question asked
- an answer that is planned, organised and well structured
- appropriate and integrated use of evidence
- appropriate vocabulary choices
- fluent and accurate control of French, construction of sentences, etc.

You will need not only to understand the plot and its characters, but to go beyond them to show a deeper understanding of the novel. To get the highest marks, you will need to be able to discuss the language and style with which the story is told, and what they demonstrate about the kind of person who is telling the story.

You will need to be able to talk confidently and in detail about the use of symbols and metaphors in the novel. You will need to be able to talk about the novel's Arab and Franco-Algerian characters in their mid-twentieth-century Algerian context, and draw on your knowledge of European colonialism to illustrate this. You will need to be able to talk about the conflict between Meursault's approach to life and the religious world view of other characters he comes into contact with, and draw on the novel's background in existentialist ideas to explain this.

These are perhaps the most challenging aspects of *L'Étranger* that you will need to get to grips with if you want to achieve the best marks, but they are not the only ones. The more aspects of the story that you are confident in writing about, the better prepared you will be for whatever comes up in the exam.

Useful phrases

To introduce your argument:
D'abord…; Je commencerai par la question de…; Je parlerai tout d'abord de…; Premièrement…; À première vue…; Pour commencer…

To link a series of points together:
D'abord…, ensuite…, enfin; Premièrement…, deuxièmement…

To introduce a new subject:
À propos de…; En ce qui concerne…; Il est important / nécessaire / essentiel de noter que…; N'oublions pas que…; Quant à…

To give an example:
notamment; par exemple

To give an explanation:
autrement dit; c'est-à-dire

To explore both sides:
D'un côté… d'un autre côté…; D'une part… d'autre part…; D'un point de vue… de l'autre point de vue…; Il est vrai que… mais…

To explain why:
parce que; puisque; à cause de

To give an opinion:
à mon avis; quant à moi; personnellement

To argue an opposite view:
cependant; par contre; néanmoins

To express frequency:
d'habitude; de façon générale; des fois; en général; fréquemment; régulièrement

To concede a point:
Bien que **(+ subjunctive)**…; En dépit de…

To sum up:
Bref…; Pour résumer…

To conclude:
Pour finir…; En conclusion…; Ainsi…

Sample questions

AS

1

Examinez l'importance de la mer et de la baignade dans le roman.

Vous pouvez utiliser les points suivants:

- la représentation de la nature • Meursault et Marie à la mer • la baignade et la liberté.

2

Meursault mérite-t-il d'être déclaré coupable et condamné à mort par la cour?

Vous pouvez utiliser les points suivants:

- les cinq coups de revolver tirés par Meursault • le rôle du hasard
- l'attention accordée à l'enterrement de sa mère pendant le procès.

3

Comparez le personnage de Raymond au personnage de Meursault. Quelles sont leurs similarités et différences?

Vous pouvez utiliser les points suivants:

- leur mode de vie • la violence • l'honnêteté.

4

Dans quelle mesure est-ce qu'on peut considérer Meursault comme un héros?

Vous pouvez utiliser les points suivants:

- le rôle de Meursault dans le complot de Raymond et la mort de l'Arabe
- l'honnêteté de Meursault • la dispute entre Meursault et l'aumônier.

A Level

1

Pourquoi est-ce que Camus appelle Meursault un « étranger »?

2

Analysez le thème de la croyance religieuse dans L'Étranger.

3

« J'accuse cet homme d'avoir enterré une mère avec un cœur de criminel. » Expliquez et évaluez cette déclaration du procureur.

4

Quelle est l'importance de l'enterrement dans le roman? Pourquoi est-ce qu'on s'y intéresse tellement pendant le procès de Meursault?

Sample answers

AS sample answer 1

Dans quelle mesure Meursault est-il responsable de la mort de l'Arabe?

Vous pouvez utiliser les points suivants:

- le rôle de Meursault dans le complot de Raymond
- l'effet du soleil et du hasard
- l'honnêteté de Meursault.

Meursault est responsable de la mort de l'Arabe parce que c'est lui qui le tue d'un coup de revolver. D'ailleurs, il tire encore quatre coups sur le corps après l'avoir tué. Il est donc vrai que Meursault est coupable de meurtre ou d'homicide involontaire. Meursault prend part aussi aux événements qui mènent à la mort de l'Arabe. Il écrit la lettre qui attire la sœur de l'Arabe dans l'appartement de Raymond, où Raymond l'agresse. Plus tard, il aide Raymond à régler l'affaire avec la police, et il participe à la bagarre avec les Arabes sur la plage.

Cependant, Meursault n'est pas responsable de la mort de l'Arabe, parce qu'il ne l'a pas fait exprès. Il est aveuglé par la lumière du soleil et désorienté par la chaleur extrême de midi. Camus écrit que 'la gâchette a cédé'. Il n'a pas écrit quelque chose comme 'j'ai appuyé sur la gâchette'. Cela montre que l'action est involontaire. Meursault n'avait pas l'intention de tuer l'Arabe.

L'explication que Meursault lui-même donne de son geste montre aussi qu'il n'est pas responsable de la mort de l'Arabe. Pendant le procès, Meursault explique qu'il a tiré 'à cause du soleil'. Puisqu'il est toujours très honnête dans le roman, même quand il est de son intérêt de mentir, le lecteur peut croire que c'est la vraie raison.

En conclusion, je pense que Meursault n'est pas responsable de la mort de l'Arabe. Meursault ne faisait pas vraiment partie du complot de Raymond contre la sœur de l'Arabe. Il l'a aidé sans y réfléchir, simplement parce que Raymond lui a demandé son aide. La mort de l'Arabe était un accident.

Better to look at reasons why he might be responsible than begin by saying that he is.

Good distinction, but could be expanded on. What is the difference between them?

Essay attempts to set up a for-and-against structure, but contradicts itself, saying first that Meursault is responsible, then that he isn't.

Good analysis of Camus's language. 'Il aurait pu écrire…' (he could have written) would have been a more sophisticated way to express this point.

Add an example here to support this point? Perhaps Meursault telling Marie he doesn't love her, or refusing to let the lawyer say he had 'dominé [s]es sentiments naturels' at the funeral.

The essay unnecessarily repeats the phrase 'responsable de la mort de l'Arabe'.

This essay takes a balanced approach to the question, looking at arguments for and against Meursault being responsible for the Arab's death. It uses lots of well-chosen evidence from the text to support its arguments, including close analysis of a quotation. However, it treats the question as if it had a simple 'yes' or 'no' answer, rather than exploring the extent of responsibility implied by 'Dans quelle mesure'.

AS sample answer 2

> Analysez le personnage de Marie. Quel rôle joue-t-elle dans le roman?
>
> Vous pouvez utiliser les points suivants:
>
> • Marie, la petite amie de Meursault
>
> • la demande en mariage
>
> • la visite à la prison.

Marie Cardona est un personnage dans le roman *L'Étranger* d'Albert Camus. L'histoire se déroule en Algérie pendant la période coloniale. Marie est une ancienne dactylo du bureau de Meursault. Il la rencontre à la plage le lendemain de l'enterrement de la mère de Meursault. Ils nagent ensemble dans la mer, puis ils vont voir un film au cinéma. Marie devient la petite amie de Meursault, puis sa fiancée. C'est elle qui propose le mariage. Il accepte, mais il lui dit qu'il ne l'aime pas.

Plus tard, Marie et Meursault entendent Raymond agresser sa maîtresse. Marie demande à Meursault d'appeler la police, mais il ne le fait pas. Marie accompagne Meursault et Raymond à la plage, mais elle ne voit ni la bagarre ni la mort de l'Arabe. Elle rend visite à Meursault en prison une fois. Puis elle lui envoie une lettre pour expliquer qu'elle ne peut plus venir, parce qu'ils ne sont pas mariés.

Marie est belle et séduisante. Elle rit beaucoup et elle est très aimable. Dans le roman, elle montre le manque d'émotion et d'empathie chez Meursault. Meursault accepte de l'épouser sans l'aimer et ne s'intéresse pas à ce qu'elle fait.

Le personnage sert aussi à montrer la vie que Meursault aurait pu avoir, s'il n'avait pas tué l'Arabe. Il aurait épousé Marie et ils auraient peut-être fondé une famille. Cependant, ce n'est pas exactement une histoire d'amour tragique. Marie prédit qu'un jour elle détestera Meursault à cause de son étrangeté.

Side annotations:

This is too basic and general. Assume your reader already knows the novel well.

Shows good knowledge of the novel, but too much story-telling and not enough analysis. What does the fact that Marie is the one to propose marriage (in the 1940s!) say about her character?

Good character portrait. Could be supported by evidence from the text.

Nice change of perspective to show how the character is used by Camus to illustrate the personality of the protagonist.

Good use of the conditional to explore what could have happened, under different circumstances.

Could be better phrased, for example: 'Son personnage fait ressortir le manque [...] par le contraste entre son caractère et celui de Meursault'.

This essay demonstrates a wide knowledge of the text and a good understanding of the character of Marie and her relationship to Meursault. It spends too long on general context and on telling the story of the novel, however, and only gets to real analysis in its last two paragraphs. This analysis is well done, explaining how Marie's character illuminates Meursault's through her contrast with him and their interactions.

A Level sample answer 1

> Évaluez l'importance du soleil dans le roman.

La plupart des événements du roman ont lieu pendant deux étés, l'été de la mort de l'Arabe et celui du procès de Meursault. En Algérie en été, le soleil est très fort, surtout à midi. Camus décrit la lumière et la chaleur du soleil en détail pendant deux épisodes importants du roman: l'enterrement de la mère de Meursault et l'assassinat de l'Arabe sur la plage. L'effet du soleil est aussi perceptible pendant le procès, à cause de la chaleur étouffante dans le palais de justice.

Avant de tuer l'Arabe, Meursault évoque la force du soleil en utilisant plusieurs métaphores. La lumière est comme 'une longue lame étincelante' qui l'atteint au front; la chaleur lui fait penser que le ciel s'est ouvert 'pour laisser pleuvoir du feu'. La description est centrée sur l'effet du soleil sur Meursault lui-même: la chaleur est comme des 'cymbales' sur son front, et 'un rideau' de sueur l'empêche de voir. L'effet est d'autant plus marqué que le style de narration de Meursault ailleurs dans le roman inclut très rarement des métaphores.

Le soleil joue un rôle très important dans l'intrigue du roman. Meursault prétend que c'est 'à cause du soleil' qu'il a tiré le coup de revolver. Son honnêteté et sa description détaillée de l'événement dans le roman portent à croire que c'est vrai. Tout ce qui se passe dans la deuxième partie du roman est donc la conséquence de l'effet du soleil sur Meursault.

Le côté philosophique du roman est aussi centré sur le rôle du soleil dans la mort de l'Arabe. Le juge et le procureur refusent d'accepter qu'un événement si terrible puisse survenir pour une raison si banale et insignifiante. Ils inventent le 'cœur de criminel' de Meursault parce qu'ils ont besoin de croire que son comportement s'explique moralement. Leur vision du monde est menacée par la possibilité que la violence et la mort puissent se produire sans raison.

Concise overview of the references to the sun in the novel. Could be expanded to mention the more positive view of the sun in beach sunbathing scenes.

Good use of quotation to support argument.

Comparison of metaphors with narrative style elsewhere is helpful to show how they stand out in the novel.

Clear structure to the answer. Four paragraphs look in turn about where the sun appears in the novel, how the novel describes it, its role in the plot, then its role in the themes.

Ambitious attempt to engage with the philosophical ideas of the novel. Could have introduced the concept of the Absurd.

This is a very well-written essay, exploring the representation of the sun from the perspectives of the plot of the novel, language and symbolism, and the novel's themes and underlying philosophy. It makes good use of quotation and other references to the text. It would have benefited from some concluding lines to sum up its views.

A Level sample answer 2

> Examinez la représentation des personnages arabes dans *L'Étranger*.

Presque tous les personnages importants de *L'Étranger*, et surtout tous les personnages dotés d'un nom, sont des pieds-noirs, c'est-à-dire des colons d'origine européenne. Les trois personnages arabes dans le roman sont la maîtresse de Raymond, son frère, qui est tué par Meursault à coups de revolver, et l'ami du frère qui l'accompagne à la plage. Nous voyons aussi le groupe d'Arabes qui suit Raymond après l'agression de sa maîtresse, dont le frère et son ami font partie, et les Arabes avec qui Meursault partage une cellule après son arrestation.

Strong opening statement with a striking fact about names in the novel.

Concise summary of the Arab characters in the novel.

Les personnages arabes dans *L'Étranger* sont souvent des victimes. La maîtresse de Raymond est humiliée et battue par lui dans une agression pour laquelle il ne reçoit aucune punition de la part de la police. Son frère est aussi battu par Raymond quand ils se rencontrent dans le bus, et il est provoqué par Raymond au commencement de la bagarre sur la plage. À la fin de la première partie du roman, bien qu'il sorte son couteau de sa poche, il ne fait aucun mouvement pour attaquer Meursault lorsqu'il est tué. Au commissariat aussi, il est frappant que la plupart des détenus sont des Arabes.

Point of argument opens the paragraph, followed by evidence and explanation.

Le lecteur a l'impression que les Arabes dans le roman sont plutôt des procédés narratifs que des personnages proprement dit. Camus écrit l'histoire d'un homme condamné à mort parce qu'il n'a pas pleuré à l'enterrement de sa mère, autrement dit parce qu'il ne 'joue pas le jeu' de la société. L'homicide de l'Arabe semble être un simple procédé pour rendre possible un procès, dans lequel l'assassinat sera vite oublié. Nous savons que, dans sa carrière journalistique, Camus condamnait l'injustice des colons envers les Algériens colonisés. Dans son roman, cependant, lui et son héros semblent partager l'indifférence et le manque d'empathie envers la population arabe qui caractérisaient la plupart des Français à l'époque.

Perspective change from looking at Arabs within the world of the story to looking at their role in the functioning of the narrative.

Contextual information from Camus's biography used as part of the argument.

Clear, personal judgment in conclusion.

This is a boldly written essay with a forthright argument which manages to remain at the same time balanced and fair-minded. It is written in accurate and sophisticated French, and makes its points clearly and persuasively. Some use of quotation from the novel as further evidence to support the argument would have been welcome.

Exam question translation

page 82

'Dans quelle mesure Meursault est-il coupable?'

To what extent is Meursault guilty?

page 84

'Pensez-vous que Raymond soit le personnage le plus immoral du roman? Pourquoi / Pourquoi pas?'

Do you think that Raymond is the most immoral character in the novel? Why / Why not?

Page 92 – AS

1

Examinez l'importance de la mer et de la baignade dans le roman.

Vous pouvez utiliser les points suivants:

- la représentation de la nature
- Meursault et Marie à la mer
- la baignade et la liberté.

Examine the importance of the sea and swimming in the novel.

You may use the following points:

- *the representation of nature*
- *Meursault and Marie at the seaside*
- *swimming and freedom.*

2

Meursault mérite-t-il d'être déclaré coupable et condamné à mort par la cour?

Vous pouvez utiliser les points suivants:

- les cinq coups de revolver tirés par Meursault
- le rôle du hasard
- l'attention accordée à l'enterrement de sa mère pendant le procès.

Does Meursault deserve to be declared guilty and condemned to death by the court?

You may use the following points:

- *the five shots fired by Meursault*
- *the role of chance*
- *the attention given to his mother's funeral at the trial.*

3

Comparez le personnage de Raymond au personnage de Meursault. Quelles sont leurs similarités et différences?

Vous pouvez utiliser les points suivants:

- leur mode de vie
- la violence
- l'honnêteté.

Compare the characters of Raymond and Meursault. What are their similarities and differences?

You may use the following points:

- *their way of life*
- *violence*
- *honesty.*

4

Dans quelle mesure est-ce qu'on peut considérer Meursault comme un héros?

Vous pouvez utiliser les points suivants:

- le rôle de Meursault dans le complot de Raymond et la mort de l'Arabe
- l'honnêteté de Meursault
- la dispute entre Meursault et l'aumônier.

To what extent can Meursault be considered a hero?

You may use the following points:

- *Meursault's role in Raymond's plot and the Arab man's death*
- *Meursault's honesty*
- *the argument between Meursault and the chaplain.*

Page 92 – A Level

1

Pourquoi est-ce que Camus appelle Meursault un « étranger »?

Why does Camus call Meursault an 'étranger'?

2

Analysez le thème de la croyance religieuse dans *L'Étranger*.

Analyse the theme of religious belief in L'Étranger.

3

« J'accuse cet homme d'avoir enterré une mère avec un cœur de criminel. » Expliquez et évaluez cette déclaration du procureur.

"I accuse this man of having buried his mother with a criminal heart." Explain and evaluate this declaration by the prosecutor.

4

Quelle est l'importance de l'enterrement dans le roman? Pourquoi est-ce qu'on s'y intéresse tellement pendant le procès de Meursault?

What is the importance of the funeral in the novel? Why is there so much interest in it during Meursault's trial?

page 93

Dans quelle mesure Meursault est-il responsable de la mort de l'Arabe?

Vous pouvez utiliser les points suivants:

* le rôle de Meursault dans le complot de Raymond
* l'effet du soleil et du hasard
* l'honnêteté de Meursault.

To what extent is Meursault responsible for the Arab man's death?

You may use the following points:

* *Meursault's role in Raymond's plot*
* *the effect of the sun and of chance*
* *Meursault's honesty.*

page 94

Analysez le personnage de Marie. Quel rôle joue-t-elle dans le roman?

Vous pouvez utiliser les points suivants:

* Marie, la petite amie de Meursault
* la demande en mariage
* la visite à la prison.

Analyse the character of Marie. What role does she play in the novel?
You may use the following points:

* *Marie as Meursault's girlfriend*
* *the marriage proposal*
* *the prison visit.*

page 95

Évaluez l'importance du soleil dans le roman.

Evaluate the importance of the sun in the novel.

page 96

Examinez la représentation des personnages arabes dans *L'Étranger*.

Examine the representation of the Arab characters in L'Étranger.

Answers

Plot and Structure

Activité 1 *(page 6)*

2. **a**2, **b**3, **c**10, **d**7, **e**8, **f**9, **g**11, **h**4, **i**12, **j**4, **k**13, **l**5, **m**6, **n**1

Activité 2 *(page 9)*

1d, 2g, 3j, 4a, 5f, 6b, 7i, 8k, 9e, 10c, 11h

Activité 6 *(page 12)*

1 sable, **2** ombre, **3** rocher, **4** brume, **5** chaleur, **6** air, **7** vagues, **8** horizon, **9** plage, **10** soleil, **11** lumière, **12** sueur, **13** rafale, **14** mer, **15** pluie, **16** ciel

Activité 14 *(page 22)*

2. **a** Je prendrai: futur simple, **b** j'arriverai: futur simple, **c** je pourrai: futur simple, **d** je rentrerai: futur simple, **e** J'ai demandé: passé composé, **f** il ne pouvait pas: imparfait, **g** refuser: infinitif, **h** c'est: présent, **i** maman n'était pas: imparfait, **j** ce sera: futur simple, **k** tout aura revêtu: futur antérieur, **l** J'ai pris: passé composé, **m** Il faisait: imparfait

Themes

Activité 10 *(page 75)*

2. **a** Raymond, **b** Marie, **c** le juge d'instruction, **d** l'avocat, **e** Meursault, **f** Meursault, **g** Meursault, **h** Céleste, **i** le procureur, **j** le procureur

the Absurd *l'Absurde (m)* in existentialist philosophy, a feeling of mismatch between the human desire to understand the meaning and purpose of everything, and the apparent lack of any meaning or purpose in the universe, seen from a non-religious perspective

atheism *l'athéisme (m)* not believing that a god or gods exist

black foot *le pied-noir* French slang term for white French settlers in Algeria during the colonial period, 1830–1962. Nobody really knows why the colonists were known as 'black feet'. One suggestion is that the term originally referred to the Algerian stokers who worked barefoot in the coal-heaps of steam-ships, then came to mean Algerians generally, and was then transferred to French people who had 'become' Algerian

blasphemous *blasphématoire* insulting, or showing contempt or lack of reverence for God

causal connection *le lien de causalité* a relationship between two events where one event causes the other

colonial *colonial* an area or country which has been conquered and is ruled by another; in this case, the Mediterranean region of Algeria was ruled by France between 1830 and 1962

colonist *le colon* a settler of a country that has been founded or conquered by the colonists' home country, or a member of a group descended from the original settlers (as is the case with Meursault)

diatribe / tirade *la diatribe / la tirade* a long, angry speech, usually denouncing or condemning something

existentialism *l'existentialisme (m)* a philosophy that humans are entirely free and must take responsibility for their own actions and choices, rejecting the idea that God or any force exists and can influence the future

first person *à la première personne* the story is told from the perspective of the main character, using the pronoun 'I' / *je*

foil *le faire-valoir* a character who contrasts with another character in a story (usually the protagonist) in order to highlight the qualities of this second character. Dr Watson is a foil to Sherlock Holmes, as Watson's simplicity highlights Holmes's intelligence. Draco Malfoy is a foil to Harry Potter, as his meanness and cowardice highlight Harry's goodness and bravery

hyperbole *l'hyperbole (f)* the use of exaggeration to create a strong impression

intermittent narration *la narration intermittente* the story is being told from a series of different points in time within the time-span of the story itself

metaphor *la métaphore* a word or phrase being used to represent or suggest something other than its literal meaning, e.g. the heart as a metaphor for love

mistress *la maîtresse* unlike 'girlfriend', this suggests a woman in a relationship with a man that is more about sex than about love, and in which she has little power and may be financially dependent. It often refers to a woman in a sexual relationship with a married man, although this is not the case with Raymond. In Camus's day, it would be seen as a shameful situation for the woman in question

nihilism *le nihilisme* a rejection of all morality, and a belief that life is worthless

nuance *la nuance* subtle differences, or shades of meaning in a writer's choice of vocabulary

omniscient *omniscient* 'knowing everything': an omniscient narrator is one who can tell us anything and everything about the characters and events of the story. Many novels have an omniscient narrator, including *Oliver Twist* by Charles Dickens and *The Lord of the Rings* by JRR Tolkien

paradox *le paradoxe* a statement that seems self-contradictory or absurd, but in fact is intended to express a truth. For example: 'Sometimes, you have to be cruel to be kind'

philosophical novel *le roman philosophique* a novel that draws on or illustrates ideas about the nature of knowledge, reality and existence (philosophy). Other famous French philosophical novels include *Candide* by Voltaire and *La Nausée* by Jean-Paul Sartre

plot device *le procédé narratif* an event or character designed to enable a plot development in the story

premeditated *prémédité, commis avec préméditation* committed deliberately, having been planned in advance (most often used with reference to murder)

protagonist *le protagoniste* the central character in a story

repent *repentir* to feel or express sincere regret for wrongdoing. The term has strong religious connotations, implying remorse for behaviour that is considered sinful

retrospective narration *la narration rétrospective* the narrator is telling us the story looking back from a point in time after the end of the story has been reached

rhetoric *la rhétorique* persuasive use of language, especially through finely crafted or emotive expressions

state secularism *la laïcité* the policy that religion should not be involved in the government or public life of a country

symbol *le symbole* something in a work of literature that stands for or represents something else, often a material object, and usually representing an important theme in the story

syntax *la syntaxe* the arrangement of words and phrases to create sentences

world view *la vision du monde* a particular understanding of the world or set of beliefs about life

OXFORD
UNIVERSITY PRESS

Great Clarendon Street, Oxford, OX2 6DP, United Kingdom

Oxford University Press is a department of the University of Oxford. It furthers the University's objective of excellence in research, scholarship, and education by publishing worldwide. Oxford is a registered trade mark of Oxford University Press in the UK and in certain other countries.

British Library Cataloguing in Publication Data

Data available

ISBN 978-0-19-841834-4

Kindle edition ISBN 978-0-19-841826-9

7 9 10 8 6

Printed and bound by CPI Group (UK) Ltd, Croydon, CR0 4YY

Acknowledgements

The publisher and author would like to thank the following for permission to use photographs and other copyright material:

Extracts from *L'Étranger* by Albert Camus © Éditions Gallimard

p46, 67, 70, 77: *L'Étranger, Préface à l'édition universitaire américaine* in Œuvres complètes, tome I, Bibliothèque de la Pléiade © Éditions Gallimard

p65, 72: *Le Mythe de Sisyphe* by Albert Camus © Éditions Gallimard

p71: Groupe Asperger d'autisme suisse romande

Cover: pmmart/iStockphoto; **p8**: Album/Superstock; **p14**: Moviestore/REX/Shutterstock; **p15**: Photostage; **p18**: Suppakij1017/Shutterstock; **p26**: Roger-Viollet/Topfoto; **p28**: NataliaMilko/Shutterstock; **p30**: Dominique BERRETTY/Getty Images; **p31**: Jean-Paul Sartre, L'être et le néant (Collection "Bibliothèque des Idées"), 1943; **p32**: Mopic/Shutterstock; **p35, 43, 65**: Jacques Ferrandez, L'Étranger, d'après l'œuvre d'Albert Camus. © Gallimard Jeunesse; **p39**: AF archive/Alamy Stock Photo; **p44**: De Laurentiis/Master/Marianne/Casbah/Kobal/REX/Shutterstock; **p48**: AF archive / Alamy Stock Photo; **p52**: Everett Collection Inc/Alamy Stock Photo; **p55**: woraput/iStockphoto; **p57**: Niloo/Shutterstock; **p73**: winnond/Shutterstock.

Every effort has been made to contact copyright holders of material reproduced in this book. Any omissions will be rectified in subsequent printings if notice is given to the publisher.